The Other Story of Lutherans at Worship

Reclaiming Our Heritage of Diversity

by

David S. Luecke

Contents

Cover photographs: Deborah Phillips
International Standard Book Number: 0-9628303-7-2

Unless otherwise noted, the Scripture quotations in this publication are from the
Holy Bible: New International Version, © 1973, 1978, 1984 by the International
Bible Society.

Chapter 1

Introduction

In 1986 about 300 participants, including me, attended a Worship and Evangelism Conference at St. John Lutheran Church in the city of Orange, California. Orange County is a kaleidoscope of many trends and changes in the country. That week end, so was St. John. It offered examples of old and new in worship, of trends toward change amidst continuity in Lutheran churches in America towards the end of the 20th century.

Founded in 1882, St. John is proud of its Lutheran heritage. At the turn of the last century, its front sign proclaimed it to be the German Lutheran Church. Still dynamic today, it has grown to be the largest Lutheran church on the West Coast. With the liturgical renewal of the 1950's and 60's, its worship order and vestments as well as music on a new organ became more refined and liturgically correct.

But a new direction began in 1985 with the arrival of senior pastor Norbert Oesch. With acceptance of the call, he had sought and received permission to be more flexible and informal with the middle of the three Sunday services. This amounted to considerable reduction in the scripted ritual (Introit, Kyrie, Gloria in Excelsis) of the traditional service, songs from sources other than the hymnal, plus a longer, expository sermon, as well as conducting the service without vestments. Soon Pastor Oesch observed a replication of the pattern he saw at his previous congregation, St. John in Bakersfield, California. By far most of the new members coming into the congregation were worshiping in the middle service, called the contemporary service.

In Bakersfield, Pastor Oesch almost "accidentally" discovered this new approach to worship. With the early and late services approaching capacity for the sanctuary, he was eyeing the Bible class time between as a place to start a third service. The change was a gradual expansion of the Bible class format. Add some songs at the

1

beginning, some prayers at the end, and turn the 40 minutes of teaching into a sermon, delivered at the front pew. Soon this was the most popular service and the one through which new members mostly came.

The music director at St. John, Orange, at the time of the conference, Mike Zehnder, also made some discoveries. A classically trained organist and choir director, he knew intimately the rich Lutheran musical heritage. But he found a new orientation when he accepted Pastor Oesch's invitation to visit some of the large Evangelical churches in the area to see what he could learn. He was impressed by the vibrancy of the music and singing along with the effectiveness of outreach to large numbers. This led him to the pivotal question, Is there anything I am doing musically that is a barrier to effective outreach? He concluded that the classical music he so enjoyed playing and presenting could be such a barrier, because it was not easily appreciated by people without a church background. Soon he undertook more contemporary emphases in his music, including a mixture of instrumentation.

The 1986 Worship and Evangelism Conference in Orange was sponsored by Fellowship Ministries, an independent parachurch organization in support of the nationwide Lutheran music ministry of David and Barbara Anderson. As of this writing they have sponsored a total of 25 such conferences across the country, attended by 4,500 Lutheran leaders. These strike me as one of the most influential ministries going on in Lutheran churches today. Experiencing is worth much more than reading or hearing about alternative worship styles.

Whatever the source of ideas, change in worship styles is happening in Lutheran churches. David Anderson suggests that in 1985 only about 15 Lutheran congregations were doing worship in a format other than that of one of the Lutheran hymnals. By the end of 1994 he and his associates estimate that number to be 3,000 - 5,000. This is out of a total of approximately 20,000 Lutheran congregations of all synods in the United States. By all indications, that number will continue to grow in the years ahead.

What should we make of this trend toward something called contemporary worship? Is it a step forward? Or is it a step, maybe two steps backwards. Is it Lutheran? These are among the basic questions for thousands of pastors and congregational leaders who are considering change for their own congregations.

Questions That Organize This Book

The plan for this book is to explore basic questions Lutheran leaders either are or should be asking as they discuss what has become a hot topic. Since the issue is forced by worship changes already happening in perhaps one fourth of all Lutheran congregations, the logical starting place after this first chapter is to ask, **2) What is contemporary worship?**

Definition is difficult because contemporary worship is evolving in many different places and comes in many different forms. This chapter will identify three formats and at least five characteristics that seem common where worship changes are underway. Terminology is difficult since the word "liturgy" figures prominently in the now-established view but finds little common agreement on its meaning. Thus I propose addressing the issue for Lutherans as pursuing classic or contemporary worship practices.

The primary characteristic of the latter is contemporary church music, which is discussed in a chapter of its own, **3) What's happening to the music?** After some description and definitions, I pursue the issue of emotions in worship and then the unavoidably fundamental question of the purpose of music and singing in worship, as understood in Scripture and Lutheran teaching.

Scripture and historic Lutheran understandings have to be basic to the whole discussion, and each receives a chapter's attention. What better place to dig in than **4) How does Scripture present worship?** Scriptural words and images for worship in themselves present definition. We have glimpses of what the early Christians did. Several writers offer standards by which they assessed worship practices.

The pivotal question underlying most current discussion is, **5) What is Lutheran worship?** The only place to find an authoritative answer is the defining 16th-century confessions that bind together Lutheran congregations and church bodies. The first one states that the classic mass of the Catholic church is retained, with some purification, but the reason why needs to be understood. The last one declares the basic, and presumably still relevant position that local congregations have the right to change "ceremonies" as they see fit. Despite all the talk about "liturgy" today, this word applied to worship is not a Lutheran concept, as will be explained in the chapter on the confessional writings.

There are two differing explanations for why Luther still talked about "the mass" in 1530. These two interpretations begin two very different stories of Lutherans at worship over the centuries—the Restoration Story and the Other Story. The Restoration Story is easy to tell because it is the official textbook one that dominates worship teaching and development in Lutheran denominational centers today. But at every major step in over 450 years of history, the Other Story presents a different interpretation, which seems often forgotten today. At least it is seldom taught.

Getting the Other Story out is the primary motivation for this book. That story's relevance to current discussions is in helping to consider the chapter-title question, **6) How representative of Lutheranism is today's dominant worship style?** In point of historical fact, the Other Story of diversity is more representative. Thus the current contemporary worship movement can be seen as reclaiming our Lutheran heritage of diversity.

The dominant Restorationists in this century have been intent on "improving" Lutheran worship. This has consistently meant more reliance on what can be called "high culture" in music and verbal eloquence. Much of the current discussion of worship practices involves differences in aesthetic or cultural tastes, with reliance on "the best" expressions to establish appropriate reverence. The Other Story has a different interpretation of reverence that has a more solid New Testament footing and that sees more value in popular culture forms. The contemporary worship movement essentially amounts to making room for popular culture expressions, especially in music style. Worship is inherently a cultural expression. This unavoidable fact forces the basic question, **7) Is there room for popular culture in Lutheran worship?**

The movement touching more and more congregations is seen as refreshing to many but as confusing, threatening, and discouraging to others. There is no simple right or wrong. Finding the most appropriate course of action for a specific congregation calls for the exercise of wisdom by church leaders. The final, summary chapter suggests **8) Reference points for wisdom in choosing worship practices.** These include restatement of theological parameters developed in earlier chapters.

Some Lutheran church leaders today can be heard claiming the contemporary worship movement amounts to a struggle for the "soul" of Lutheranism. This view simply does not square with Scripture or the defining Lutheran teachings. In technical terms, worship practices are "adiaphora," things neither commanded nor forbidden. There is plenty of room for diversity. Worship practices are the wrong part of church life on which to force unity.

The right basis for unity is doctrine. While there is no guarantee against flawed understandings in any group of pastors, there is nothing approaching consistent evidence that Lutheran pastors leading contemporary worship are challenging or forsaking Lutheran doctrine. Unlike previous church-wide issues in recent decades or in the mid-19-th century, this one is not a doctrinal dispute. It is about wisdom for putting received doctrine into practice.

The true "soul" of Lutheranism is the centrality of justification by grace through faith. Lutherans, by theological necessity, have always resisted legalism in any form. Restoration advocates, intentionally or inadvertently, often seem to advocate what amounts to liturgical legalism. When that kind of pressure is on, the only true Lutheran response is to resist and to exercise the freedom in worship taught by Scripture and the Lutheran confessions.

Lest there be any doubt, the purpose of this writing is not to argue that one form of worship is inherently better than another. Churches face differing circumstances and have differing emphases in mission. **The intent is to make the case as convincingly as possible that there is room in authentic Lutheranism for a <u>diversity</u> of worship styles.** That's why it tells the Other Story of Lutherans at worship, the one that reclaims our heritage of diversity. Such diversity can be a strength for a church body, not a weakness.

Chapter 2

What Is Contemporary Worship?

Contemporary worship is a movement touching churches of many denominations. Among Lutherans it is sometimes called alternative worship. As with most movements, it does not yet have a precise definition.

But there are clues. You are probably in a contemporary worship service when a few or more of the following things happen:

- The singing is being led by 3 or 5 people up front with microphones in their hands.
- Song words are projected on a screen for all to see.
- The pastor is not wearing a gown. Or in churches where a suit is the norm, the pastor is wearing a sport shirt.
- Very little the pastor or congregation says is read from a script.
- The music is done with an ensemble of synthesizer or piano, guitars, and maybe a few other instruments. The organ is probably not used at all.
- When there is a drummer and drumset, you know for sure you are in a contemporary worship.
- Some of the songs have just one verse that is sung over and over again. These are called choruses. They are often woven into medlies.
- A number of participants help lead before the service is over.
- There is clapping during the singing and perhaps at other times.
- As a visitor, you do not feel too conspicuous.

These are only clues, not a definition. Contemporary services come in all sorts of combinations of new with old, since such worship in a congregation usually evolves out of its traditional practices, many of which often continue with increased appreciaton for their strengths.

Formats

The format for contemporary worship varies considerably. What follows are observations for Protestant churches in general. These tendencies can be seen in Lutheran churches as well.

Perhaps the easiest format to understand is the expanded Bible class. The Introduction described one pastor's development of this approach by turning the Bible class time between the early and the late service into worship by adding some songs at the beginning and prayers at the end. The relative informality of a class carried forward, and the singing was of songs easily appreciated. The preaching, in Bible-class style, is called expository.

A very different format is the seeker service. This is approached as a time for outreach to seekers who may not have made a Christian commitment. The service has to be especially interesting to attract these unchurched people and to hold their attention. The emphasis is on relationships—leading into and from the relationship with Christ. The message is direct and simple, addressing people's felt needs and avoiding theological language. The entire service is planned to be non-threatening to the audience, with no calls for commitment or money. Frequently dramas portraying everyday life struggles are presented, and perhaps a short, direct testimony is given. Scripted ritual is almost non-existent.

The music at a seeker service is decidedly contemporary, ranging from Christian rock to country and western. The intent is to be similar to the music these people most commonly listen to. Participants are not asked to sing often, on the assumption that the unchurched crowd has very little experience with group singing. Thus, the singing is done for them, and high standards of quality and impact are set for the soloists and musical group.

It is quickly apparent that a seeker service is very different from a traditional Sunday morning worship of almost any Protestant heritage. Sometimes this is called pre-evangelism. Another term beginning to appear is entertainment evangelism. Typically a church that offers a seeker service will have another more conventional service at another time as well as more conventional educational programs for the members who have made a Christian commitment. The seeker service is not intended to carry the whole life of the congregation.

The church most visible in pioneering a seeker service approach is Willow Creek Community Church in a northwest suburb of Chicago. From a beginning only 25 years ago it now has a Sunday attendance over 10,000. The members have their more conventional worship, including periodically the Lord's Supper, on Wednesday evenings.

The Lutheran church most visible in using this approach is the Community Church of Joy in Phoenix, Arizona. Their worship attendance now averages about 3,000. The connection between a seeker service and large attendance accounts for much of the widespread interest in this very non-traditional approach to worship.

Yet another format takes a very different approach toward music. The music itself is still contemporary, but it is meant to be sung by all as acts of worship rather than to be presented by a few to silent listeners. Praise and worship singing is the name given to this approach. Songs are merged together into medlies that may go on for 10 to 15 minutes. Praise choruses are the name for many of these simplified songs, but medlies may also include traditional hymns. This movement towards an extended time of singing is happening across many Protestant denominations.

Contemporary worship services can have all sorts of formats that blend together some or most of these distinctive elements. For many churches, substituting praise choruses for hymns left in their traditional places in the order of worship constitutes contemporary. The Lord's Supper may be celebrated on the same schedule it was in traditional worship.

In almost all contemporary worship there is a tendency to simplify what happens during the time together. In some churches, simplification tends to reduce the frequency of celebrating the Lord's Supper.

Some Lutheran churches that are pace setters for contemporary worship in one form or another are Prince of Peace in Burnsville, MN (ELCA), St. Johns in Ellisville, MO (LCMS), King of Kings in Omaha, NE (LCMS), Calvary in Golden Valley, MN (ELCA), Salem in Tomball, TX (LCMS), Grace in Huntington Beach, CA (ELCA), Christ the King in Fallbrook, CA (ELCA), Faith in Troy,

MI (LCMS), Advent in Boca Raton, FL (ELCA), and First Trinity, Tonawanda, NY (LCMS).

Characteristics of Contemporary Worship

Recognize the following characteristics as common to these formats and initial impressions .

1. Contemporary worship features contemporary music.

2. Contemporary worship is typically visitor friendly.

3. Contemporary worship emphasizes informality for the sake of good communication.

4. Contemporary worship usually features revitalized preaching.

5. Contemporary worship tends to feature many different leaders who stand in front and face the congregation.

1. Contemporary worship features contemporary music.

Reliance on music composed in recent decades is the key characteristic of contemporary worship. This topic is big enough to merit a chapter of its own, which follows. In preview, this music tends to have emotionally expressive melodies, more syncopated rhythms, and an absence of the four-part harmonies of traditional hymns. They tend to be single-verse choruses that are repeated and are often woven together into medlies. A variety of instruments—more than a guitar and without organ—is typically used to support the singing.

The other four characteristics are related one way or another to the rationale that leads to reliance on contemporary music.

2. Contemporary worship is typically visitor friendly.

Worship traditions have a way of accumulating and getting more complicated among Christians who worship together regularly and learn specialized rituals and songs that become routine. Over time their worship can become so specialized that visitors have a hard time understanding and appreciating the flow of the service. The event does not become a time of worship for them.

In Lutheran churches, the 1960's and 70's were a time of considerable attention to a movement called liturgical renewal, which concentrated on recovering worship ingredients and practices used extensively in previous centuries, especially the sixteenth and, better, the fourth centuries. The movement culminated in the publication of the *Lutheran Book of Worship* in 1978 (now the standard in the Evangelical Lutheran Church in America) and then the very similar *Lutheran Worship* in 1982 (now used in about half the congregations of the Lutheran Church--Missouri Synod).

In addition to being new for everyone, these settings were more complicated in terms of presenting options and alternatives from which choices had to be made in a specific service. Many worship leaders concluded that these new settings were not designed with the visitor in mind. Thus there has been a small movement to reproduce in the worship folder just the options used on a specific Sunday. The new technology of computerized word processing in the church office facilitated this customizing. Once the Sunday service is individually reproduced weekly, simplification and substitution of components follow easily. Worship leaders became accustomed to designing every worship service. Those for whom the needs of visitors were clearly in focus could design, and usually simplify, accordingly.

That the needs of visitors rose in importance is one of the effects of a movement of a different sort in the 1980's in Lutheran churches. Church Growth is the common name for new ways of thinking about church and ministry that found adherence in many Protestant denominations. These are the ones, including Lutherans, which had to confront the fact that numeric growth in membership was no longer occurring as it had in almost all Protestant denominations in the 1950's and 1960's. The great majority of their congregations were experiencing numeric decline.

Church Growth thinking itself remains controversial, although less so now than a decade or so ago. A survey by *Leadership* journal, a quarterly for congregational ministers, shows that across Protestantism ministers have reduced their resistance to Church Growth concepts and approaches and are more willing to incorporate them into their leadership. Among Lutherans, one can observe that pursuit of church growth studies, principles and applications is more prevalent among pastors and denominational leaders of the LCMS than those of the ELCA.

The reason for referring here to the Church Growth movement is simply to note the very high overlap between an interest in contemporary worship and an interest in Church Growth approaches. In most basic terms, common sense says that church leaders who are purposeful about pursuing numeric growth of a congregation will pay extra attention to visitors and their needs. They will begin to look at all the congregation does, even its worship, through the eyes of visitors, or as it is sometimes called, through church-growth eyes. They will be receptive to changes in worship that will help visitors to understand and appreciate what is happening. Increased exploration of contemporary worship is a natural result

Clearly the question of for whom worship is planned becomes central to controversies surrounding contemporary worship in Lutheran churches. Because of the proud ethnic heritage of most such churches, they are not used to looking beyond the gathered congregation to those who do not yet share the heritage.

Another similar tension point concerns the frequency of celebrating the Lord's Supper in regular worship. The liturgical renewal movement featured weekly celebration of this sacrament as proper worship. Indeed, all of the Sunday worship settings of the new hymnals feature communion as the norm, with the option of skipping several pages to end without communion. Anything else is called "alternative" worship, which is a name used by many to cover what is here called contemporary worship.

While the Lord's Supper will always be celebrated regularly in any church claiming to be Lutheran, one can safely say that it is observed less frequently in contemporary worship settings than in services following the new Lutheran hymnals. Greater concern for the needs of the visitor is one explanation, since communion is usually understood as a service for those who have a clear Christian commitment and indeed a commitment to the Lutheran church. Another explanation is the general concern to simplify the regular worship

Yes, we claimed it was right, now know we were wrong, but compromise for the sake of unchurched

service. There is ample historical precedent. For most of the 475 years of Lutheranism, communion was not celebrated weekly; for centuries the norm was quarterly, and for much of this century it was monthly.

Thus current tensions have to do in part with an earlier movement toward greater frequency and elaboration in celebrating the Lord's Supper meeting new interests in visitors as part of a movement toward greater simplicity in worship.

To determine what is properly Scriptural and Lutheran will require whole chapters later. Until you, the reader, get to them, here are a few observations about the issues of visitors and simplification. When the Apostle Paul corrected the worship practices of the Corinthians, he stated the principle that their worship should be done so that when a visitor ("an unbeliever or someone who does not understand") comes he "will fall down and worship God, exclaiming 'God is really among you'." (1 Cor 14: 24, 25)

proof for choice based on content

In his study *Luther on Worship* Vilmos Vajta observes that Luther saw the need for flexibility in worship. "All his liturgical reforms betray his concern for the spiritual well-being of the weak in faith. They needed a form of service which would provide for their edification without being bound to a single pattern"[1] According to the Lutheran Confessions: "The community of God in every place and at every time has the right, authority, and power to change, to reduce, or to increase ceremonies according to its circumstances." (Formula of Concord, Solid Declaration, Article X, paragraph 9[2])

Few Lutheran churches pursuing contemporary worship eliminate traditional worship in its favor. Most offer both, at different times on Sunday morning. Thus the issue need not be which is the "best" form of worship. The question is whether to support diversity in meeting differing needs.

3. Contemporary worship emphasizes informality for the sake of good communication

One of the key objectives of the contemporary worship movement is to improve communication with the participants. This has implications not only for the sermon but also for the whole style of interaction between worship leader and congregation. Informality is a characteristic of that style.

The opposite of such informality is scripted ritual which is read by both the leader and the people. In the orders of service featured in the new hymnals, every word that is spoken or sung is written either in the hymnal or a special resource book used by the leaders. Frequently the sermon is the only part of the service not scripted in detail, and sometimes in this approach the preacher may tend to stay close to reading the message written for that service.

The advantage of this formal approach is that everyone knows what to expect and the utterances are typically well crafted and even elegant. The service progresses in a predictable and orderly fashion that reduces chances for distraction and is reassuring and comfortable.

The disadvantages come from the negative side of predictability. The flow can become so familiar that they no longer register upon consciousness. Simple repetition by rote can let thought content go by without registering on the participants. Thoughts wander and personal engagement with what is happening may lessen. The boredom of deadening sameness is often not far behind for those who find themselves slipping into a mental absence from what is going on. A 19th-century English pastor and author, George McDonald notes, "Nothing is so deadening to the divine as an habitual dealing with the outsides of holy things."[3]

Communication studies suggest that the more predictable something is, the less impact it will have on our consciousness. In commenting on the matter of familiarity and predictability Eugene Nida of the American Bible Society uses the term "information" to describe data which registers at a deep motivation level. While he speaks to issues of translating Scripture, the principle is relevant also to worship. He says, "A fundamental principle of information theory is that the amount of 'information' carried by any item is directly proportionate to its unpredictability. In other words, if we can predict the occurrence of a particular word or expression, then that word carries very little 'information' or impact."[4]

One dimension of informality is a sense of spontaneity. Something may happen, perhaps even in just a small way, that is not anticipated. Formality stresses having a protocol or rite for everything, usually by writing everything out ahead of time, thus reducing the chances of the unexpected. Proceeding without a script does not assure spontaneity, but it at least opens the door and even invites the unexpected. Such a possibility helps maintain attentiveness.

James White, a former president of the North American Academy of Liturgy and a professor of liturgy at the University of Notre Dame, notes that early Christian worship involved spontaneity. This can be seen in Paul's discussion in 1 Corinthians 14. White comments on the inherent difficulty of planning to include spontaneity, "which ebbs and flows as the spirit moves and is not subject to the medium of print." He sees it nevertheless as an important ingredient of worship. Dependence on service books works against spontaneity. He says, "But it should be clear that worship and service books are by no means synonymous. Service books can only provide standard formulas. A healthy balance must remain between such formulas and the unwritten and unplanned elements that only spontaneity can provide."[5]

Another dimension of informality can be seen in the dress of both worship leaders and participants. Visit a church that has both a traditional and a contemporary service and you can usually see a preponderance of suit and tie and "Sunday" dresses at the traditional service, and a preponderance of sports shirts and slacks or even shorts at the contemporary service. Folks at the former are likely to see worship as something "otherworldly" and different from everyday activity; more formal dress is appropriate. Folks at the latter are likely to view "everydayness" as important to authentic worship; more informal dress seems fitting.

The mode of dress carries over to worship leaders. Typically in contemporary worship the pastor and other leaders, like the worship team, will not wear gowns. For Lutherans this means the pastor wears a suit (with or without clerical collar, but typically without).

In Lutheran churches, clergy clothing fashion for worship has changed several times in recent decades--an argument for the constancy of change in worship. Some fifty years ago most wore a simple black gown, perhaps with a little white bib. In the 1950's and 60's there was a strong movement toward a black cassock with a white surplice over it--something reminiscent of Catholic (and Lutheran) worship leaders about the time of the Reformation. Then in the 1970's and 80's the shift was to a white gown called an alb--a simplified style fashioned on the fourth century. Now the cutting edge of worship is to the relative informality of no special gown at all.

Informality is relative. Recently I was discussing worship with a pastor from a large Nazarene church I had visited several years earlier. He said they, too, were "going contemporary." I asked what that could mean, since the worship I had witnessed earlier (including song words on a screen overhead) already seemed contemporary by Lutheran standards. Music, of course, was part of the change. But he also explained that after the early "traditional" service, the pastors would change from suit and tie and come back in sports shirts to lead the "contemporary" worship.

4. Contemporary worship usually features revitalized preaching.

Since effective communication is one of the primary objectives in contemporary worship, this concern naturally carries over to preaching. There is increased attention to the basic simplicity of Scripture and application. For some this means expository preaching, letting a text unfold into application. For others this means starting with felt needs of the listeners, like personal insecurities or difficulties in relationships, and then applying Scriptural insights. The emphasis on good communication leads to heavy use of stories and illustrations to capture and hold interest, getting back frequently to practical applications. At a minimum, higher priority is given to avoidance of boredom. While these emphases are not unique to contemporary worship, more time and attention are likely to be given to them when "going contemporary."

Just the differing amounts of time given to the sermon are instructive. As the liturgical renewal movement focused more attention on the Lord's Supper as a major component of every service, the normal length of the sermon tended to decrease. This was partly due to less time available in the usual one hour service. But is also reflected greater reliance on the sacrament as the place to encounter God. Thus the usual recommendation is to aim for 12-15 minutes of sermon.

As the emphasis on effective verbal communication increases, so does the need to have more time to do that. Illustrations, stories, and applications take time to develop, especially if the message is to build from Scripture and get beyond the obvious and the superficial. Sermon lengths in contemporary worship typically would be more like 20-30 minutes long or more. This "message" time may include a 5-10 drama to gain attention and provide focus.

From his experience, the dean of current Protestant church observers, Lyle Schaller, provides guidance to answer the question, How long should the sermon be? His answer is, "It depends..." Much of the answer depends on the skills of the preacher, the design of the sermon, and the expectations of the people. Here are a few reference points he suggests:

- The best oral communicators can hold an audience's attention for 75-90 minutes. For speakers with slightly above average skill, the ceiling is closer to 25 minutes.

- If the people gathered are motivated mostly by institutional loyalty, guilt, social pressure, or habit, the sermon probably should not exceed 15 minutes. If they come expecting their religious needs to be addressed, their spirit nurtured, and their lives enriched, 35-75 minutes may be appropriate--if the sermon accomplishes this.

- The greater the proportion of the congregation who came after years of no active participation in a worshiping community, the longer the sermon can be.

- Preachers who read from a manuscript are advised not to exceed 15-20 minutes. Those who preach with few or no notes may allocate 20-40 minutes.

- The more distant the speaker is from the audience, the more difficulty there will be capturing and holding attention. "Thus the minister who comes down out of the chancel and delivers the sermon while walking among the people has a substantial advan-

16

tage over the preacher in a pulpit that is at least 15 feet from the closest parishioner."[6]

Pressure for improved communication skills in church abound as participants are saturated with written, oral, and visual messages from the media that surround them. One way to address that competition is to lean toward withdrawing from it and relying on well known tradition to carry the communication, even if that means depending on one of its least effective forms, the repeated reading of written scripts.

The other approach is to take on the challenge to communicate as well as the competition. This leads to an openness to easily understood, fast moving variety and application in spoken message. Getting and holding the participants' attention is as important in what is said as it is in presenting the music. Leaders who pursue contemporary worship tend to follow the logic of better communication in their preaching, too.

5. Contemporary worship tends to feature many different leaders who stand in front and face the congregation.

Traditional worship, especially for Lutherans, tends to have only the pastor and perhaps several assistants "in front," that is, in the chancel. Perhaps lay readers of scripture will come forward for that part. Music tends to come from behind, with the organist and choir, if there is one, typically in the balcony. The rationale is that keeping the music makers out of sight enables worshipers to concentrate on the words and music without being distracted by persons.

Again, concern for good communication leads to putting anybody exercising leadership where eye-contact can be maintained—the leaders with the participants, but perhaps even more important, the participants with the leaders. Much can be expressed both ways that goes beyond the words and the musical notes. The informality permits especially music leaders to alter what they are doing or saying in reaction to the congregation's response. The desire for greater flexibility is one of the reasons, by the way, that contemporary worship often does not have a big choir, even when the congregation has one for traditional worship. Another reason is that typical choir anthems, performed separately, can break the flow of participation in singing.

Furthermore, anybody with anything to say or sing will usually wind up not only in front of the people but also in front of a microphone. The implication for good communication is obvious. Amplification can also fill the room with stimulating sound even when congregation singing is weak. As churches start taking contemporary worship seriously, they soon find themselves investing in an upgraded sound system, usually centered on an expensive mixer that controls a dozen or more microphones and sources of sound. This then calls for a new kind of worship leader--the sound mixer who controls the equipment. This is the one function that stays in back out of sight.

Contemporary worship also may have attention-focusing drama in the service, and this of course happens in front. The range of activities with many different leaders places new demands on space. In effect, the balcony where the music was made gets transferred to the front--along with the clutter of stands, etc. usually found there. To this is added the clutter of microphone cables and various sound apparatus. Just the appearance of what is in front of them can be a source of tension between traditional worshipers with expectations of formality in the chancel and contemporary worshipers whose sense of informality keeps them tuned to function more than symbols. Annual placement of the Christmas trees has a way of increasing the tension over space and appearance.

As a reflection of the changed perspective on space, consider the sanctuary renovation recently done at Royal Redeemer Lutheran Church in North Royalton, Ohio. In addition to pastoring the neighboring mission congregation, Community of Hope, I serve as administrative pastor there, and this role has placed me in the middle of facilities planning. Steady growth in attendance, almost totally related to the mid-morning contemporary service now in its fourth year, is pushing the limits of sanctuary, classroom, and fellowship space. One project was to redo the chancel to better accommodate all the 'up front" activity of the contemporary worship. At the same time, the intent was to leave as much as possible the current appearance for the traditional first service.

The current Royal Redeemer sanctuary was built 25 years ago and incorporates well designed liturgical symbolism in the chancel. The altar, a simple table, is close to the front wall. Were this redesign happening 10 years ago, the almost automatic recommendation would be to bring the altar far out from the wall so it would be more the center of attention and the pastor could officiate from behind it. Now, it was moved but just enough for the pastor to get behind it occasionally. The primary concern is to have as large a platform as possible free for flexible use. The pulpit, font, and lectern were made more portable so they can be moved around as needed. The pulpit basically is not used in the contemporary service, since the speaker stands as close to the congregation as possible, typically by the front pew. The worship team fits better in the area where the pulpit is, so everything fits better if the pulpit can be pushed aside for that worship time.

Contemporary worship is more than substituting a newer kind of music for traditional church music. It brings a shift in the way a number of functions of leadership in worship are done, and these changes have ripple effects.

Those ripple effects are worthy worrying about. Church tradition and symbols should be approached with respect and care. But a time of change usually refocuses attention on function more than on form. Usually, such refocus is healthy.

Scope of Contemporary Worship in American Churches

Contemporary worship is a movement affecting many Protestant denominations beyond Lutheranism. Some data can help describe the scope and characteristics of the movement as of 1994. Consider the results of a survey done by *Your Church* magazine reported in the March/April 1994 issue. Their questionnaire was sent to a random selection of American churches of all denominations. It focused on the proportion of Sunday music that was "traditional" without stating definition. Half the churches were thus described as traditional (75-

100% of the worship music is traditional), one quarter as moderately traditional (50-74% traditional music) and one quarter as non traditional (reporting that less than 50% of the music is traditional)

Here are some observations that add perspective to what is happening to contemporary (nontraditional) worship in American Protestantism in 1994.

- There is no difference in average Sunday attendance between traditional and less traditional churches.
- Non-traditional churches have a significantly higher attendance in proportion to membership (85%) than predominantly traditional churches (58%). This last percentage should be compared to the 30-40% attendance characteristic of Lutheran churches.
- Traditional churches are less likely to have grown in the last five years. While 38% of traditional churches grew more than 1%, the percentage for less traditional churches was a higher 54%.
- Traditional churches tend to have older pastors. The proportion of pastors over the age of 50 in traditional churches was 47%. In moderately traditional churches the percentage over 50 was a lower 31%. In non-traditional churches it was an even lower 21%.

Terminology

The article from *Your Church* just cited reflects one of the difficulties talking and writing about recent changes occurring in worship. Those authors chose to key off the word "traditional" and then distinguish lesser amounts of it.

Contemporary in contrast to traditional is the distinction used so far in this book. This does seem to be close to common usage among church leaders feeling their way into the subject at hand.

What are the alternatives? One sometimes hears the new contrasted to "liturgical" worship. A Lutheran church near me proclaimed on its sign that "liturgical worship" was at 9:00 and "contemporary worship" at 11:00.

But this distinction shows a shallow understanding of liturgy. This term seems best used to describe planned public worship. Thus any purposeful planning of public worship yields a liturgy. While in common usage the term is usually applied to extensively scripted rites and rituals, such formality is not essential to the definition. A productive distinction addressing the issue at hand would be between "formal" liturgy and "informal" liturgy. Or maybe describe the traditional liturgy as "classic". Thus one can talk about classic liturgy and contemporary liturgy.

Advocates of classical liturgy have a way of claiming the whole word for themselves. Thus a call to arms emblazoned on T-shirts at one Lutheran seminary proclaims "Join the resistance! Support the liturgy!". They mean the classically scripted public worship that, in addition to the Word and prayers, features the Lord's Supper and includes such classical components as Introit, Kyrie, Gradual, Preface, Sanctus, Agnus Dei and appropriate collects.

Liturgical scholar James White notes that using "liturgy" in the narrow sense of the Eucharist comes from Eastern Orthodoxy. He adds, "Western Christians use 'liturgical' to apply to all forms of public worship of a participative nature."[7]

In the chapter on the Lutheran Confessions, we will note that the Formula of Concord makes the same reference to origin of the narrow usage in Eastern Orthodoxy. But the main point of the confessors' discussion is that liturgy is not the preferred vocabulary. Confessional terms are "ceremonies" and "practices." In current discussion neither side would rush to claim the historic term "ceremonies." Perhaps we would do well to distinguish simply between classic and contemporary worship practices.

Summary

Always a challenge, effective communication has become especially difficult in the face of the sophisticated print, audio, and video messages that saturate our daily environment. The liturgical renewal movement of the 1950's - 70's had many objectives, but effective communication was not high on the list. While that thrust brought more visual stimulation through symbols and garments, those symbols tended to be static and to require learning to appreciate. The expansion of ritual forced reliance on the least effective oral communication—reading from a script.

21

One way or the other, the main characteristics of the contemporary worship movement have evolved from efforts to improve communication of the Gospel to an audience assumed to have newcomers still finding their way into church. Thus contemporary worship typically:

a) is visitor friendly.

b) emphasizes informality.

c) features revitalized preaching.

d) seeks face-to-face, attention-holding contact between leaders and congregation.

And, of course, contemporary worship features contemporary music. That topic leads into the next chapter.

---

[11] Vilmos Vajta, *Luther on Worship: An Interpretation*, Muhlenberg Press, 1958, p 180.

[2] *The Book of Concord: The Confessions of the Evangelical Lutheran Church*, trans. and ed. by Theodore G. Tappert, Muhlenberg Press, 1959 p. 612.

[3] Robert H. Mitchell, *I Don't Like That Music,* Hope Publishing, 1993, p. 29.

[4] Ibid, p. 29

[5] James F. White, *Introduction to Christian Worship,* Abingdon Press, 1980, p 31.

[6] Lyle Schaller, "The Parish Paper," Naperville, Ill., May 1994.

[7] White, op. cit., p. 24.

Chapter 3

What's Happening To The Music?

The synthesizer is a distinctly modern instrument. It is a long narrow box with a board of musical keys. Deceptively simple looking, it can produce an unlimited variety of sounds through the computer inside, coupled to electronic amplification. It can be a piano, or an organ--and a lot more. The instrument is often known as the keyboard, and the player is the keyboardist.

The synthesizer is the dominant musical instrument used in contemporary worship. It represents change in more than just technology. It is also the dominant instrument in most forms of contemporary music wherever performed--in shows, in bars, on recordings. The sounds produced are often very similar to those heard in popular entertainment. Whether you think this fact is good or bad for worship will reflect much of your attitude toward contemporary church music and contemporary worship. If you expect the Sunday church experience to be very different from any other experience, the organ, preferably a pipe organ, is to be much preferred. If you are looking for the Sunday experience to relate to everyday life, the synthesizer in church is welcome.

Whatever your answer, though, you should know another impact of the synthesizer, or keyboard. Youthful interest in serious study of the classical organ has dropped precipitously in preference to the keyboard. Organ majors in college-level schools and departments of music have declined dramatically. And the study of organ almost automatically translates into music leadership in a church. Knowledge and performance of the classical organ repertoire will almost certainly diminish in the years ahead, even at churches where the desire for traditional church music remains high.

Music alone does not explain all the differences between contemporary and traditional worship. But it explains more than any other single factor.

Toward a Definition

Another modern innovation, this one economically driven, makes possible a working definition of contemporary church music. The pursuit of composer royalties for music notes and words still under copyright protection is done much more seriously now than even a decade ago. Most churches now have copyright licensing through Christian Copyright and Licensing Incorporated (CCLI), which has emerged for collecting and distributing royalties. Surveys that meticulously count songs used and their frequency are necessary to make the system work. One result is the availability of a fairly accurate report on the copyrighted songs used in churches. In most cases the music repertoire is contemporary, since such church-by-church protection and reporting is usually not sought for traditional hymns in traditional hymnals.

As a result of copyright surveys, we now have listings and rankings of songs according to their popularity in actual church worship usage. Table 1 presents the top 25 reported by churches to CCLI for the period of October 93 to September 94.

It was just a matter of time until a publisher put out a collection of the current top songs in one volume. Word Music did this in its 1992 publication *Songs for Praise and Worship*, containing 253 of the most popular contemporary songs used in church worship.

This volume can serve as a reference point for the discussion that follows. "Contemporary" church music can cover almost anything, from rock to country western to modern classical. Much of it is for solo activity, and this sort is difficult for congregational singing. In the Word Music collection, actual congregational use is the basic criterion for selection. Few of the songs in this collection could be considered rock, and few are country western. The name emerging to describe them is "Praise and Worship."

The editors present this definition of a contemporary praise and worship song: "Simply stated, it is a congregational song that usually incorporates contemporary harmonies and rhythms. Its lyric usually utilizes a first person expression of praise to God for who he is.... The melody supports the heart of the lyric by its emotionally expressive contour and design."[1]

Table 1

Top 25 Songs Reported by Churches to Christian Copyright Licensing, Inc.

1.	"He Has Made Me Glad"	Leona Von Brethorst
2.	"I Love You Lord"	Laurie Klein
3.	"Give Thanks"	Henry Smith
4.	"Majesty"	Jack Hayford
5.	"As The Deer"	Martin Nystrom
6.	"Glorify Thy Name"	Donna Adkins
7.	"We Bring the Sacrifice"	Kirk Dearman
8.	"Jesus Name Above Names"	Naida Hearn
9.	"All Hail King Jesus"	Dave Moody
10.	"I Will Call Upon the Lord"	Michael O'Shields
11.	"This Is The Day"	Les Garrett
12.	"Awesome God"	Rich Mullins
13.	"I Exalt Thee"	Pete Sanchez
14.	"Praise The Name of Jesus"	Roy Hicks, Jr.
15.	"How Majestic Is Your Name"	Michael W. Smith
16.	"Open Our Eyes Lord"	Bob Cull
17.	"Lord, I Lift Your Name on High"	Rick Founds
18.	"Holy Ground"	Geron Davis
19.	"He Is Exalted"	Twila Paris
20.	"Emmanuel"	Bob McGee
21.	"Lord Be Glorified"	Bob Kilpatrick
22.	"Great Is The Lord"	M. W./D. Smith
23.	"His Name Is Wonderful"	Audrey Meier
24.	"Seek Ye First"	Karen Lafferty
25.	"O How He Loves You and Me"	Kurt Kaiser

In these songs rhythms are characteristically more syncopated than the straight beat of traditional hymns. Especially the praise music tends to have a pronounced beat that lends itself to hand clapping. The "emotionally expressive contour and design" of the melody means that it is usually easy to learn and remember. "Powerful" is another word for the effect the melody can have on those singing it.

The most evident difference in harmonies is the less frequent appearance of the four-part harmonies of traditional hymns. In this Word Music collection, only 53 out of the 253 songs in the congregation's version contain four-part harmonies for the complete song or even in part. One of the simplest ways to distinguish contemporary from traditional church songs is in the left hand accompaniment.

Another characteristic of these songs leads to naming them choruses rather than hymns. Most in this collection have only one verse. Only about one quarter (60 out of 253) have more than one verse, and usually the additional verses change only a word or two.

What does one do with a song having only one verse? Sing it over several times. The first time gets the melody established and the repetition allows meditation on the words. Some churches may sing a chorus 15 to 20 times, but two or three times is much more the norm. A skillful worship team changes each repetition a little in intensity, or accompaniment or key; modulations up by half steps are common as a way of refreshing interest.

A test I like is to have a group sing three verses of the well-known traditional hymn "All People That On Earth Do Dwell" to the very traditional tune Old Hundredth, and then sing the contemporary "Bless the Lord, O My Soul" three times. Both are songs of praise. Then I ask participants to summarize in a sentence the sentiment they expressed in each song. There is 100% recall of wanting to bless the Lord, but the memory of the point of the three-verse hymn is usually rather hazy.

This example reflects a significant difference of purpose between the two types of church song. The traditional hymn features a text in poetic form that usually offers instruction as well as expression. The music is almost a neutral carrier of words; in fact, hymn tunes of the same meter are often interchanged.

A contemporary chorus focuses completely on expression of feeling and sentiment, and the melody becomes an integral part of that expression. Implicit is the assumption that the fewer the words the more focus there can be on their meaning. These songs are not just about praise and worship. Singing them is itself primarily an act of praise and worship.

The definition cited earlier highlighted the first-person statement--"I" or "we"--of these choruses. This facilitates the act of personal worship, moving beyond instruction. In most cases, these choruses are in the first person singular rather than plural. The risk of a loss of sense of community certainly exists by foregoing the "we," but the "I" does underscore the personal nature of this expression.

Across various Protestant traditions, the most typical pattern of songs in church services is to have three hymns--one at the beginning, one before the sermon, and one at the end. Each might have three to six verses.

A tendency in contemporary worship is to cluster the songs together, typically at the beginning of the service. They become medlies, with one song flowing into the next and the next, and so on. A medley usually would have three or four songs but might extend to seven or even ten.

There are two dynamics at work here. One is an increased appreciation for variety. In our fast-paced media environment people increasingly tend to find their attention drifting if it is not refocused on something slightly different. One can usually observe how energy wanes by the sixth stanza of a hymn. Changing melody and meter is refreshing and helps refocus.

The second dynamic is simply extending the amount of time in singing at one time. Music touches the heart as well as the mind. Variety addresses the mind. Duration addresses the heart, or the emotions. For most people the emotions are engaged gradually and cumulatively. One can almost envision layers of engagement. Thus it helps to have the melody of choruses support the thought of the lyric by its "emotionally expressive contour and design." Extended time in song is important for the cumulative effect of the flow of melodies in addition to the changing lyrics. A well constructed medley will aim at moving the participant through various postures of both head and heart. That is much more difficult to do if the singing is broken by extended periods of speaking.

At work in this cumulative effect are some fundamental dynamics of brain functions.

Left-Brain, Right-Brain and Whole-Brain Worship

Brain research offers a fundamental distinction in brain functions that helps explain what is evolving in contemporary church music. The human brain clearly has two halves. The left hemisphere controls logical reasoning and language skills. The right hemisphere shows a definite correlation with affective (emotional) and intuitive patterns of thought and spatial perception as well as with music production and appreciation and also religious mystical experiences.[2]

Much of the time, the left hemisphere tends to dominate in daily functions. But not always. Some people are distinctly right-brain oriented, and many can move with ease back and forth in dominance of one or the other. Generally a person for whom one half is totally and consistently dominant will have difficulties in relating to a variety of people, coming across as either coolly rational and dispassionate or as irrationally emotional and resistant to reason. Most people most of the time operate somewhere in-between these extremes, with the left brain typically dominating most of the time.

Insights from brain research have application to two issues of church music today. The first relates to preference for extended medlies versus scattered single hymns. Within characteristic dominance of one hemisphere, there is still typically a cycling between the two halves that in relation to each other increase one cognitive style for awhile and decrease the other. Some research suggests a full cycle of about 90 minutes.

Since sensitivity to music is a right-brain function, music will have greater impact the more the right hemisphere comes into relative dominance. Longer participation in music exercises the right brain more and can bring it into dominance. But, also, because of the normal slight cycling between left and right hemispheres, an increased amount of time participating in music in itself increases the probability that the right brain will swing into dominance and the experience will become more emotional. This dynamic helps explain why some churches develop a period of praise and worship singing that extends to 30-45 minutes.

The second issue is whether worship practices should even try to provide for a period of right brain dominance. You might think providing music of any sort constitutes an appeal to the right brain. Indeed, some church traditions (like Churches of Christ--Non-Instrumental) have sought rational orientation by significantly curtailing music of any sort. But even within the broad range of music used in churches, some is distinctly more left-brain oriented. Gregorian chant is noted for its cool cerebral character, aided by a lack of melody. Much of the music of J. S. Bach, too, can be considered left-brained oriented, with its precise, controlled, contrapunctal arrangements.

Several considerations point to an easy affirmative to delibereate appeal to the emotional right brain, but there are additional considerations that provide complications.

In a truly random collection of people, there will be a significant proportion who are characteristically right-brain dominant. To offer a time in a worship service oriented especially to their needs seems sensible and considerate. The rational functions of reading and listening to the spoken word typically appeal to the left brain, and differences in dominance help explain why some hearers get much more (or much less) from a sermon than others. Even for those whose dominance is more balanced, shouldn't there be a time to exercise the emotional, intuitive right hemisphere—the part stimulated, for instance, by emotionally expressive melodies and a pronounced beat?

Whole-brain worship is advocated by Dieter Mueller, a Lutheran minister in the Vancouver, British Columbia area whose 1989 Ph.D. dissertation addressed brain hemispheres and spiritual experience. He sees a heavy dependence on left-brain functions in traditional, especially Lutheran worship. One of the consequences is decreased effectiveness in ministering to more emotionally oriented right-brain-dominant people, who will tend to withdraw from situations that leave unfilled the needs they see important because of their personality. Mueller goes on to suggest that baby-boomers typically are more right-brain oriented than their elders because of their long exposure to the distinctly right-brain, visually and musically oriented communication medium of television and to a much more rhythmic music diet. The cultural shift in communication precipitated by television in itself calls for reassessment of worship practices.

One might observe, by the way, that the opposite exclusion also happens. Left-brain oriented Christians will tend to become uncomfortable with highly emotional church service experiences where rational control seems disregarded. This excess seldom is a problem for Lutheran churches. Yet Christians whose entry into Christian faith and church life has been through Pentecostal or charismatic experiences and who are ready to move on typically do not find their way to traditional Lutheran worship. They, like right-brain dominant Lutherans, would look for a balance that provides for both rational structure and emotion. This can be called whole-brain worship.

Dieter Mueller provided for this present writing some provocative although preliminary data from ongoing research relating output of brain activity to listening to traditional hymns versus listening to contemporary choruses. For all subjects (both right- and left-brain dominant) the alpha brain waves measured higher in output when listening to contemporary upbeat, more rhythmic songs than when listening to traditional hymns. Such increased engagement of attention in itself would for many be a persuasive reason to increase use of contemporary songs in worship.

Overagainst such pragmatic considerations, we need to recognize an underlying issue which would call into question any deliberate attempt to stimulate right-brain activity. Appeals to subjective emotions are strongly suspect in many traditions of Christian worship, including now-prominent strains of Lutheranism.

Fear of excesses is one readily understood basis for this resistance to emotional music. Emotions without constraint of reason can lead to actions that are more damaging than constructive to the individual as well as to the community.

But even within moderate bounds, some leaders resist appeals to emotions because the response can seem to many so undignified and inappropriate in solemn worship. King David experienced this reaction to his very right-brain emotional dancing as he led the procession carrying the ark into Jerusalem. His first wife, Michal, shamed him for this vulgar behavior of a commoner. But David was not worried about dignity; he wanted to celebrate before the Lord and that meant expressing his emotions in dance and the music fitting for it (2 Samuel 6: 14-22). Psalm 150 was very fitting for David's worship: Praise God with trumpet, harp and lyre, tambourines and dancing, string and flute, and the clash of cymbals.

Many churches today, Lutheran as well as others, would be very wary of David's style of worship. In general you will find more openness to it among those attracted to contemporary worship than those favoring the classic tradition, which is so much more "reasonable" and easier to explain. Perhaps this just means that over time left-brain-dominant worship planners tend to prevail.

Anyone who has difficulty recognizing a place for emotions in worship will almost inevitably find contemporary worship music unappealing and perhaps even unacceptable.

The tension between reason and emotion, left-brain and right-brain worship music, forces the question of the purpose of church music. Whether what's happening in contemporary music is good or bad ultimately has to take into account the view of its purpose in worship.

To Praise or To Teach?

Distinguish between worship (whole service) and teaching. Worship -praise Teaching - sermon, scripture

Listen carefully to talk about worship in churches with extended periods of singing and you can often hear the term used differently than in traditional churches. "After the worship" doesn't mean after the whole church service is over. When, for instance, announcements will be made "after the worship," this means when the singing is finished and before the Scripture is read and expounded. In this usage the service has two main parts--worship and teaching. In some churches these are equal halves in the time devoted to each.

In this usage the purpose of the music and singing is simply to praise and worship God. This is a time for adoration and thankfulness. Within this purpose there is even a subtle difference, to be discussed in the next chapter, between praise music and worship music. In terms of the classic liturgy, much of contemporary church music is an expansion and elaboration of the Gloria Patri, the Gloria in Excelsis, and the Sanctus.

In contrast, traditional hymn singing serves more of a teaching function, especially in the Lutheran heritage. Messages about God and Christian living are set in a poetic form and receive the support of a melody to help sustain attention. A good sermon hymn, for instance, presents a theme that then receives spoken elaboration. Unlike contemporary choruses, virtually all traditional hymns have more than one verse in order to deliver a fuller, more complete message. From the teaching perspective, it makes sense to sing all the verses; stopping after only a few leaves an incomplete teaching and itself suggests a shift in purpose from the traditional one. *length often my time than by teaching.*

agree Done too

31

Within this teaching purpose, the melody seems more a neutral carrier of words. Several different tunes of the same meter can be and often are used for the same text; selection is usually done on the basis of which is better known or easier to sing. Or different texts can be set to the same tune. For instance, a popular Lutheran hymn melody "O Welt Ich Muss Dich Lassen" began as a secular song first published in 1488, "Innsbruck, I Must Leave You," It shows up published as a spiritual song in 1506 with "O Welt" (O world) substituted for the city Innsbruck. In *Lutheran Worship* it has three sets of text: "Arise and Shine in Splendor" by Martin Opitz in the early 17th century, "Upon the Cross Extended" by Paul Gerhardt in the mid-17th century, and, also by him, "Now Rest Beneath Night's Shadow."

In contrast, contemporary songs of the sort in *Songs for Praise and Worship* are usually composed with words and melody closely intertwined. It is hard to imagine a given melody used to support a different set of words. Perhaps in a future generation, after copyright has expired, someone will try. But such effort will be difficult because most of the melodies do not have an easily identifiable meter. The melody is much more than a neutral carrier of words; in the best of contemporary worship music it becomes an expression of the sentiment of the words. For instance, one of the currently most popular songs (fifth among the top 25) is "As the Dear Panteth," composed by Marty Nystrom in 1984. He described his method as starting with Psalm 42 in front of him, meditating on the words, and then developing different melodies until he found the one most expressive of the worship he was trying to express.[3]

What should be the purpose of singing in a church--to praise or to teach? With one-verse choruses and truncated hymns, the use of songs as acts of a praise and worship relationship with God is on the rise. This is seen in much more use of the first and second person variations on the theme: Because you (God) bless me so richly, I offer you (God) my praise and proclaim my love for you. The teaching hymns are typically in the third person—about God and about those who would follow him.

A greater awareness of the difference between purposes occurred to me one Sunday after we had a third-person didactic hymn in our medley. An affirming woman observed that she didn't want to sing the sermon; she would rather have it preached to her, and leave the singing as a time for praise. That is far from a superficial criticism easily brushed off.

An easier criticism to handle comes from worship leaders with a song-as-teaching agenda who point out the textual inadequacies of this or that popular chorus as presenting a shallow or incomplete message. Certainly "Bless the Lord O My Soul" is very simple. (Repeat the first line and add "and all that is within me bless his holy name.") So is "Glorify Thy Name." (After "Father, we love You, we worship and adore You," sing "glorify Thy name in all the earth" three times. Repeat all this addressing Jesus and a third time address the Holy Spirit.) Simple, yes. Simplistic? That depends on the attitude and self understanding the singer brings to this act of worship. In any event, both are as straightforward and potentially profound as a Gloria Patri.

Yes, many contemporary praise and worship songs fall short of a full Christological message, or do not present a good reminder of sin and justification. But that is not the intent. There are other parts of the time together, chiefly the sermon, for the full message. *They are praise, not teaching times.*

good pt!

The Purpose of Church Song
in Scripture and Luther

For many Lutherans, the teaching function of church song will not be diminished so easily. A counter argument is to claim support from Scripture that Christian songs are to serve the purpose of teaching. In Colossians 3: 17 Paul encourages those Christians to "Let the Word of God dwell in you richly in all wisdom; teaching and admonishing one another in psalms, hymns, and spiritual songs, singing with grace in your hearts to the Lord." So states the King James version. The NIV, however, connects the psalms, hymns and spiritual songs to the act of singing as a third way of letting the Word dwell richly, alongside teaching and admonishing. As usual in such variance the Greek text is ambiguous, and the split scholarly opinion detracts from the persuasiveness of the narrow didactic view. In the larger scope of the whole Scripture, the evidence is overwhelming that temple and synagogue worship featured singing for the purpose of offering praise. This would have been the heritage of the early Christians.[4]

What about Lutheran heritage? Is the hymnody oriented to teaching by theological necessity or simply by custom? A later chapter will concentrate on the understanding of worship in the Lutheran Confessions. But two passages speak directly to the issue at hand. In the Large Catechism's explanation to the Third Article, Luther clarified that one of the reasons to "sanctify the holy day" was that people have opportunity to participate in public worship, "that is, that they may assemble to hear and discuss God's Word and then praise God with song and prayer."[5] It is interesting to note this dual understanding of Sunday assembly supports the same simple two-fold order emerging in churches that pursue extended praise and worship singing. For people continually in the Word, the reverse order of praise first and then teaching need not detract from seeing this worship time as thankful response to remembrance of God's initiatives. The worship serves as good warm-up preparation for focusing on God's Word.

This narrower understanding of worship in distinction from learning is also presented in Article 15 of the Apology of the Augsburg Confession as part of the illustration for how good discipline is maintained: "The children chant the Psalms in order to learn; the people sing, too, in order to learn or to worship."[6]

Perhaps there is a broader theological position inherent in good Lutheranism that overshadows these passing Confession comments recognizing worship activity different from receiving teaching. In recent generations, Vilmos Vajta presents the most comprehensive study of Luther on worship based solidly on the Reformer's theological presuppositions. Vilmos observes that "Luther developed his theology of worship along two lines, as he proceeded either from his picture of God or from his concept of faith....The strength of Luther's theology lies in his keeping both of these ideas in view."[7]

Some interpreters of Luther express the focus on God as the "pedagogical view," which considers worship "an institute of the mature in faith for the training of the immature"—something done to strengthen and deepen the faith of the believers.[8] The counter view, which focuses on faith, would see worship as "the believers' common sacrifice of praise," and the church service is seen as an offering of praise to God by the faithful.[9]

Lutheran dialogue on worship was carried on in the 19th century around the distinction between an objective and subjective picture of the church and worship. Objective and subjective are still used in discussions of worship today. One current, officially endorsed position declares the dictionary definition of worship as human response to God as "antithetical to the Evangelical Lutheran understanding of worship," which is proclaimed to be just the opposite in seeing worship as coming from God to us.[10] This very proper emphasis on the the objective Word and sacraments, which are to be proclaimed, taught, and administered, seems to suggest that the subjective faith response of thankfulness and praise is unimportant. *Important*

This latest de-emphasis on the subjective becomes one more interpretation that opts to simplify and break the tension in the unity of both objective and subjective that Vajta sees as basic to Luther's understanding. Vajta cites an array of Luther passages to support the position that "true worship is an expression of faith in prayer, praise, and thanksgiving. It is the reflection of the 'mood of ownership,' so characteristic of the faith of the early Christians and of Luther."[11]

To repeat, there is a dualism in Luther's theology of worship. On the one hand church and worship appear to be identical with the proclamation of the Word and the administration of the sacraments. On the other hand, church and worship appear to be the work of faith, where worship is not just for training and strengthening faith but also for the worshiper's expression of his faith. "This dualism in Luther's theology," according to Vajta, "is the reason for the wide divergence among his interpreters."[12] *Both/And, not either/or*

Summary

These last few paragraphs may seem much heavier than necessary to answer an apparently simple question: Is it OK in authentic Lutheran worship to sing simple praise and worship songs that fall short of teaching the full message of sin and salvation in Christ? A reasonable answer is Yes, assuming other parts of the service present Law and Gospel proclamation.

Because of Luther's dualism, others may disagree and insist on a one-sided emphasis. As I will show also in subsequent chapters, there has always been plenty of room in Lutheranism for diversity. For now, recognize that even in the theology of worship there is room for diversity of emphasis and style. To insist otherwise simply contradicts the facts.

Meanwhile, it is possible to plan without a guilty conscience Lutheran services that focus singing on expressing praise and worship and leave the preaching and teaching for other parts of the service. Certainly there will be pragmatic concerns in a specific congregation. But so long as Law and Gospel are somewhere proclaimed in the service, there is no theological reason to prevent the shift in style represented by Praise and Worship music.

---

[1] *Songs for Praise and Worship: Worship Planner Edition,* Word Music, 1992, p. 446.

[2] P. Bakan, "Two Streams of Consciousness: A Typological Approach," in J. C. Singer and K. B. Pope, *Streams of Consciousness: Psychological Iinvestigations,* New York: Plenum, 1978, pp. 159-184.

[3] Marty Nystrom in lecture presentation at Fellowship Ministry worship workshop in Phoenix, Arizona, January 1993.

[4] J. C. McCann, Jr., "Song," *The International Bible Encyclopedia,* ed. G. W. Bromiley, Eerdmans, Vol 4, p. 582.

[5] "The Large Catechism (1529)," *The Book of Concord,* trans. and ed. by Theodore G. Tappert, Muhlenberg Press, 1959, p. 376.

[6] "The Apology of the Augsburg Confession (1531)," *The Book of Concord,* op. cit., p. 220.

[7] Vilmos Vajta, *Luther on Worship: An Interpretation,* Muhlenberg Press, 1958, p. 18.

[8] Ibid., pp 20, 125.

[9] Ibid., pp. 20-21.

[10] Roger D. Pittelko, "Corporate Worship of the Church," *Lutheran Worship: History and Practice,* ed. by Fred L Precht, CPH, 1993, p. 44.

[11] Vajta, op. cit., p. 125.

[12] Ibid., p. 143.

Chapter 4

How Does Scripture Present Worship?

Consider these possible situations. How would you go about answering the question for each?

A church has two worship services. At one the singing is led by an organ and at the other by several guitarists. Which is better worship?

Three people are singing the Gloria in Excelsis. For one it is new, and she is concentrating on getting it right. The other has sung it hundreds of time and does it flawlessly now, but his mind wanders as he does so. A third is not singing at all. Who is most engaged in worship?

One group sings praise songs and prays together for about an hour. For the same amount of time another hears pastor-led Scripture readings, sermon, and prayers. Which is better worship?

In one service people come dressed up and stand, sit, or sing only as directed, and they are usually quiet. In another the dress is more casual; some stand while others sit and a few hold up their hands; the mood is boisterous. Where is more worship happening?

How would you answer these questions? Can they be answered? Is the quality of worship reflected by demeanor or excellence of presentation? Or is it reflected more by inner attitude or attentiveness? Can there be worship without the Word of God or without participants' heartfelt response to that Word?

What, basically, is worship? A simple question. It is the fundamental question for issues of worship in churches today.

Yet there is no simple answer. The many traditions of worship in Christian churches today stand as testimony to differences in emphases, even among Biblically-centered churches. Controversy over contemporary worship is a symptom of but another round of ferment in this area. New attention to something so basic as worship is bound to be healthy and productive in churches.

This chapter will pursue three approaches toward useful understanding. The emphasis is on useful, because the starting point is live congregations which for an hour or so on Sunday morning are moving beyond what is currently understood as traditional Lutheran worship. The end result needs to be guidance in how do that faithfully. This chapter identifies faithfulness to God's expectations as set forth in Scripture. The next one explores faithfulness to Lutheran Confessions and traditions of church life.

The first approach is to identify how Scripture presents worship in general. The second looks for glimpses of how the early Christians worshiped. The third focuses on the meaning of biblical criteria for the planning of worship today. Planning is the issue at hand. After all, even traditional orders of service in a hymnbook are only plans for what is supposed to happen. The rightful question is whether such a plan, or any other, is effective in bringing about the desired worship. Simply saying the words is no guarantee that worship results.

We need to do this well!

Before plunging in, consider this thought provoker from W. Nichols:

> Worship is the supreme and only indispensable activity of the Christian Church. It alone will endure, like the love for God which it expresses, into heaven, when all other activities of the church will have passed away. It must therefore, even more strictly than any of the less essential doings of the church, come under the criticism and control of the revelation on which the Church is founded.[1]

I. Worship in General

Worship is a word that loses much of its real meaning in democratic, everybody-is-equal American culture. The substance of its meaning in Biblical culture revolves around dimensions of submission. Where submission to someone else was a part of everyday life, worship was easier to understand.

Worship as Bowing and Complimenting

Some Biblical word pictures can help bring the concept alive today. In the Greek New Testament and the Greek translation of the Old Testament, the word most commonly translated "to worship" is *proskynein*. In the general literature of that time this verb described the widespread oriental custom of bowing and even prostrating oneself before another, such as a king, as an expression of respect and submission. Thus when you hear the word "worship" today, you can rightfully think of the act of bowing before God.

In some church traditions kneeling reflects this submission. Many Lutheran congregations still follow the custom of communion recipients bowing to the altar before they receive the elements in the Lord's Supper.

When you get lost in thinking about worship, call to mind first of all <u>posture</u>-- the act of bending over before the Lord as an expression of submission and respect. Today some worshipers acknowledge submission by raising their hands over their heads—a present-day posture of surrender.

Now add another element to the picture. The one who was in the posture of submission usually said something after bowing. The words that come naturally would be about how great and important the other one is, the one to whom respect is being given. We today would say, give a compliment. The Biblical words were much more robust. Their expressions were praise—strong statements of respect for the other's characteristics and actions.

Thus, picture Abraham's servant, sent to find a wife for Isaac, when he recognized that his prayer was wonderfully answered: "The man bowed down and worshiped the Lord, saying, 'Praise be to the Lord, the God of my master Abraham, who has not abandoned his kindness and faithfulness to my master'." (Gen 24:26) From the beginnings of worship by God's people go to one of the last scenes in Scripture. In John's vision in the fourth chapter of the Book of Revelation, the Lamb seated on the throne is surrounded by 24 elders. They "fall down before him who sits on the throne and worship him who lives forever and ever... and say: 'You are worthy, our Lord and God to receive glory and honor and power, for you created all

things and by your will they were created and have their being'."
(Rev 4: 10-11)

That's worship!

Those words, "You are worthy," are very significant. They lead to the English words most commonly used to translate *proskynein*—worship. The word developed from the Old English for worthy. Literally worship means worthship--ascribing worth to someone else.

Now focus on that act of ascribing worth. If we dig a little deeper into the basic Greek word we can came up with yet another dimension of worship that is perhaps easier to grasp in today's culture. After all, the bow has pretty well disappeared in social interaction, having been replaced by the more egalitarian handshake. Asians still practice the bow, and Americans typically get confused about how to respond, a situation that perhaps parallels some of the current confusion about worship.

That root word *proskynein* is a compound of *pros*, meaning 'toward" and *kynein*. Of all things, the second part literally means "to kiss." Probably the term came into use to describe the act of bowing toward and kissing the feet of the other. Kissing today is well recognized as part of a different kind of act of ascribing worth to someone, that is, as part of expressing love. A man in love with a woman is sometimes described as worshiping the ground she walks on. Being 'in love " with someone is to submit one's will and even independence to that person. The words of love naturally lead into describing the worth of the other. For instance, in old versions of the marriage service of the Anglican Book of Common Prayer the husband's promise is, "With my body I thee worship."

Admittedly this next point is pushing the image of *proskynein*. But the approach to worship as a love relationship is gaining in recognition in contemporary understanding of church worship. The Scriptural base is readily apparent: "You shall love the Lord your God with all your heart, with all your soul, with all your mind and with all your strength" (Mark 12:30). Jesus himself describes this as the most important part of our relationship to God. To love God is to worship. To worship God involves expressions of a love relationship, just as it involves a relationship of bowing submission.

There is something called the "praise and worship" movement within the larger movement of contemporary worship. Churches are sometimes described as rediscovering praise and worship. In such use, those are not two words that mean basically the same thing. Worship is taking on a narrow sense focused specifically on expressing a love relationship with God, with a sense of quietness and soft words of adoration. Two songs epitomize this narrow sense:

> I love You, Lord, and I lift my voice
> To worship You, O my soul rejoice!
> Take joy, my King, in what You hear:
> May it be a sweet, sweet, sound in Your ear.
> Laurie Klein

******

> Worthy, You are worthy, King of kings,
> Lord of lords, You are worthy;
> Worthy, You are worthy, King of kings,
> Lord of lords, I worship You.
> Don Moen

In an increasing number of churches today, a time of worship now typically describes a medley of singing that progresses from a loud, brash, energetic, festive celebration of God's greatness and majesty to quieter moments of more serene, contemplative and tender adoration from the hearts of those who have drawn near.

One of the leaders of this movement, Don McMinn, who has a doctorate in church music, suggests that the personality of praise is joyful celebration, and the sounds of praise should resemble a pep rally.[2] He points out that the primary Hebrew word for praise, Halal, means to boast, to shine, to be clamorous, to rave, to make a show, to celebrate. Psalm 150 is the clearest expression of such clamorousness, as all the various instruments join together. Try thinking of fans welcoming back to their city the victorious baseball World Series champions. This is praise in action.

McMinn describes the progression from praise to worship this way: "As we see Him from a distance, we applaud Him and boast with loud shouts of praise and joyful singing; and as we draw near, we become enthralled with His presence and we worship him with songs and words of love and tenderness."[3]

Worship as Reverent Awe

Perhaps for you the image of Christians gathered in church for a pep rally of praise may seem too rough and boisterous, and the image of love songs of submissive worship to God may seem a little too tender. What does this do to reverence? Doesn't worship involve a sense of awe and fear of God as someone wholly other than us?

Reverence is the word most usually used to describe the special sense of respect and honor to God that is traditionally expected in church worship. Reverence means giving honor by wearing your best clothes—your Sunday best—and by special eloquence in prayer and song, by cool refinement in manner. As a boy, I learned that reverence means no talking, or running, or wearing a cap in church.

Probably the major criticism of contemporary worship by those looking from the vantage point of tradition is that it lacks "reverence."

So let's look at reverence as part of a general understanding of worship. But let's do it from the starting point of a conclusion by Biblical scholar David Peterson in his Biblical study of worship: "When Christians imply that reverence is essentially a matter of one's demeanor in church services, this shows little understanding of the Bible's teaching on this subject!"[4]

Peterson points out that in the Greek of Bible times there was a common word used extensively to express the notion of reverence, respect, and honor for the gods. *Sebomai* also came to be used to describe reverence given through organized worship, or cultic activity.

But that word, *sebomai*, is simply not used in the Bible to describe favorably the worship of God's people. It appears twice in the Greek version of the Old Testament in relation to worship of God's people, but not worship that is commended. In the New Testament it is used of non-Christians or as an accusation by non-Christians.[5]

Peterson argues that when the notion of reverence is used favorably in Scripture it describes the general sense of reverence or fear of God expressed by attitude and lifestyle: "Reverence and respect for God is essentially a matter of walking in his ways and keeping his commandments."[6] In the New Testament a different word is used to describe the notion of fearing God, and always in the

42

sense of relationship and lifestyle. That word is *phobos*, meaning fear. It is available in English as phobia, or the fear of something, like the fear of high places, or acrophobia.

Let's stay with the concept of phobia, the word most often translated as reverence or reverent in the New Testament. It has the negative connotation of fear, and that is why "fearing and loving God" just does not seem to go together to the modern ear. The more positive side is awe, as being in awe of a hero. It is possible to be in awe of someone you love. This is the fundamental meaning of reverence for God. The challenge is how to fear God without being afraid of him.

If reverence is going to be used as a reference point for Sunday Christian worship (which, as noted, is not done in the Bible for worship services specifically) then the full meaning of the word should be appreciated. It describes an emotion, most readily recognized as fear mixed with awe in relation to someone. It should lead to looking for an emotional response of those involved in worship. This is something much more profound than formal, well-dressed and well-rehearsed decorum and elegant words associated with traditional worship.

It is possible for most participants in worship to observe all the traditional proprieties of reverence and still not have true reverence for God. This is especially so for worshipers who come to depend on the outward markings of clothes, symbols and action and who through familiarity over time lose the emotional response of awe. Likewise it is possible for participants in everyday clothes and informal interaction to have profound reverence in sung, spoken and inner response to God. Of course, the opposite in each case may also be true.

Biblically, there are two tests for reverence in worship. Do participants reflect a relationship to God that has emotions of awe? Do participants exhibit attitudes and life styles of submission to God and his ways? Thus reverence is tested as much by what happens during the week as by what is done for an hour on Sunday.

The matter of lifestyle leads into a third perspective on worship in general.

Worship As Service To God

The newer Bible translations (NIV, TEV) present yet another dimension of worship in general. In Romans 12:1 Paul urges us to "offer your bodies as living sacrifices, holy and pleasing to God--this is your spiritual (reasonable) act of <u>worship</u>" (NIV). Any discussion of worship has to take this passage into account and with it the Greek word translated as worship--*latreuein*.

Let's go back to the starting image of bowing and expressing compliments, or showing submission and expressing praise. Once such recognition is given, the next natural step is to offer something or do something to express respect and submission. To do service is such an act of worship. Sometimes in the Greek Old Testament the word used to describe such worshipful service to God is the service of a slave. It is not just doing nice things for God. The worship Paul is talking about is a lifestyle of submission to God's will.

Let Jesus clarify the relation between worship and doing: "Worship (*proskenein*) the Lord your God and serve (*latreuein*) him only" (Matt 4:10).

This sense of service in relation to worship is important to recognize because of one of the terms commonly used to describe the special hour of congregational worship on Sunday—a church service. Lutherans especially need to be aware because the basic German word for that hour is *Gottesdienst*--divine service. *Gottesdienst* is a wonderfully ambiguous term; it can mean God's service to us and also our service to God. Without doubt, authentic worship has to have God's initiative to which we respond. But the Biblical use of *latreuein*, or service, clearly describes our service to God.

Liturgy

[handwritten note: need more on this - too cursory for such an important word, at least from today's Lutheran perspective]

One other potential Biblical image for worship needs to be recognized. This is *leiturgia*, from which we get the word liturgy so much in use today. The word in the Greek Old Testament has frequent use in Old Covenant cultic worship with priests and sacrifices.

Of the 15 New Testament uses of this terms, six occur in the Book to the Hebrews. Their use in that book is instructive, because the word is consistently used in association with Old Testament worship. The basic point of the New Testament Book to the Hebrews is that the prescribed rituals and priestly representation (the "cultus," as worship specialists like to call it) have been fulfilled in Jesus Christ and no longer have separate relevance to the relationship of God and his new covenant people. All the important categories of the Old Testament approach to worship—sanctuary, sacrifice, altar, priesthood, and covenant—are taken up and related to the person and world of Jesus Christ. The writer proclaims the end of that earthly "cultus" by proclaiming Christ's work as its fulfillment.

Thus Hebrews hardly commends *leitourgia* for Christian worship. The other New Testament uses stay close to the literal meaning of the term—the public work or service of the people. They describe, for instance, the service of supplying the needs of God's people and the needs of Paul in particular (2 Corinthians 9:12; Philippians 2:30). The only reference to something resembling what we would consider a worship service is in Acts 13:2, where the Holy Spirit spoke to the church in Antioch about sending Paul and Barnabas on their first missionary journey "while they were worshiping the Lord and fasting." Considering the next verse, the meaning seems to be spiritual preparation by praying and fasting.

Here is the conclusion H. Strathman reaches from his exhaustive study of *leitourgia* in Scripture: "Movement toward a new Christian use occurs only in Acts 13:2 with reference to prayer. The end of the Old Testament cultus with Christ means that the terms are not suitable for the functions of Christian ministers.... The new community has no priests; it consists of priests, for all can enter the sanctuary through Christ's blood."[7]

So how has liturgy come to be almost synonymous with worship in recent Lutheran discussions? This is a recent development, by the way. As you will see, the term receives discussion only in a short section of the Lutheran Confessions, as basically a footnote, and then the confessors distance themselves from a specialized use for worship.

We can find a clue through an observation by worship scholar James White. He notes that "the liturgy" is used in Eastern Orthodox churches to describe the specific sequence of ritual in celebration of the eucharist. But Western Christians have used "liturgy" and "liturgical" to apply to all forms of public worship of a participatory nature.[8] We can add to this the observation that Eastern churches would have maintained use of the Old Testament in Greek, and there *leitourgia* appears regularly in relation to the prescribed priestly cultic activities. Their elaborate ritual celebration of the eucharist tends to become a continuation of the Old Testament priestly sense.

So, "doing the liturgy" is not a New Testament notion of worship. As we shall see in the next chapter, it is not a Lutheran one either. If it is to be used in Western culture, it should describe any form of public worship of a participatory nature. But even there, let it be recognized that the word is devoid of Christian theological meaning in relation specifically to worship.

"Techniques of public worship" is probably the most neutral and safest understanding of the word "liturgy" today. But the word has acquired heavy emotional overlays of specialized understandings. In this writing, the preference is for more direct Scriptural and confessional vocabulary.

II. Structured Congregational Worship

Now let's turn from worship in general to the specific hour of Sunday worship. It is indeed Sunday church worship that is the basic subject at hand. But whatever goes on in that hour should at some point and in some way be reflective of worship in general—individuals expressing their submissive relationship to God in attitude, words, and action. The heading "structured congregational worship" is a deliberately neutral term.

The task now is to let Scripture add meaning and content. Our starting point is what the early Christians did when they gathered to worship. Remember, a basic point of the New Testament Book to the Hebrews is that the prescribed rituals and priestly representations of the old covenant have been fulfilled in Jesus Christ and are no longer binding in the relation of God and his new covenant people.

This starting point of the early Christians needs comment. As will be developed in the next chapter, basic to Lutheran understandings of worship is that rites, ceremonies, and practices are adiaphora, meaning matters of indifference that are neither commanded nor forbidden in Scripture. Thus some Christians may well choose to adopt Old Testament images and vocabulary for their worship; they have this liberty so long as what they do presents and responds to Christ. Others may well choose to key off Christian worship practices in the fourth century or some other century.

Yet for many Christians, myself included, what the first several generations of Christians believed and practiced is a more compelling reference point than accumulations of values and practices added in later centuries. The wellspring for Christian church life today remains what the New Testament writers, under inspiration, present of the church of their time. Stated another way, given a choice of worship practices, I would prefer to stay close to the current equivalents of doing things the way the early Christians did. This seems especially important in times of turmoil over defining worship expectations.

The New Testament writings provide only a few windows on what happened when these early Christians gathered for worship. The biggest and clearest is Paul's reaction to what the Corinthian believers were doing when they gathered for worship. This is in 1 Corinthians 11-14. Perhaps another window is the short description of the immediate and instinctive actions of the very first Christians called together on Pentecost, as recorded in Acts 2: 42-47. Otherwise we have some slight glimpses in subsequent chapters of Acts and a short reference in Hebrews 10.

Some activities are so apparent they need little comment here. The Word was preached and taught. The early believers gathered in temple courts and houses, where the apostles "never stopped teaching and proclaiming the good news" (Acts 5:42). When the apostles were getting distracted by arrangements for the gathering, they chose to concentrate on "prayer and ministry of the Word" (Acts 6:4). In Ephesus Paul carried on daily lectures and discussions with the people for two years (Acts 19:9-10). Among the believers gathered in

Troas, Paul "spoke" for hours (Acts 20:7). These were not twelve-minute sermonettes!

Those who gathered in the name of their Lord prayed. This is frequently mentioned as part of events that were not necessarily worship. Certainly it happened then, too. And certainly prayer included praise, something inherent in the notion of worship the Jewish Christians carried with them.

Because of troubles that emerged in the worship of the Corinthians, Paul opens two windows on their practices. Sometimes when they came together, their purpose was to eat (1 Cor 11:33), and this eating included celebration of the Lord's Supper, the name Paul used for it. They needed to understand the spiritual nature of this eating and drinking, and they had to figure out how to avoid letting it be divisive.

The next window is three chapters later. Here he says when they come together, "everyone has a hymn, or a word of instruction, a revelation, a tongue or an interpretation." Two activities are most apparent. They sang, and they gave and heard instruction in God's Word. These parallel Paul's admonition to the Colossians to let the Word of God dwell in them richly "as you teach and admonish one another with all wisdom, and as you sing psalms, hymns, and spiritual songs with gratitude in your hearts" (Col 3: 16). The ambiguity about whether psalms, hymns, and spiritual songs go with teaching or singing was discussed in the previous chapter, with the conclusion that at least the Jewish Christians would have grown up singing praises.

While explicitly allowing for the additional possibilities of someone speaking in tongues (14:39), Paul rather clearly discourages it in the assembly (14:27,28, also 3,18,19). The reason becomes an important criterion for planning worship—that visitors can understand what is happening and recognize the presence of God.

Whether what happens in the congregational worship of Chapter 11, that is, the Lord's Supper, also happens at the congregation worship described in Chapter 14 is an open question. In other words, we have no clear evidence that every time they gathered to worship they also ate together and celebrated the Lord's Supper. Verse 33 in

Chapter 11 suggests otherwise, in focusing just on a time when they gather to eat.

Some commentators would regard Acts 2:42 as a window on the four elements basic to the gathered worship of the very first Christians: "They devoted themselves to the apostles' teaching, and to the fellowship, to the breaking of bread and to prayer." This would imply instruction, table fellowship, then the Lord's Supper and prayers.

There are several difficulties for using this passage to outline worship, however. One is that the following verses expand on the initial summary and look to activities that took place at different times and different places. The other is that the term "breaking of bread," probably refers to little more than eating meals together, since that is the thrust, for instance, of verse 46 ("They broke bread in their homes and ate together with glad and sincere hearts.") Sharing regular food is a big part of what they routinely did, as evidenced by the need for more leaders to "wait on tables" (Acts 6:1-2). "The fellowship" probably refers to all the close-knitness of sharing they did, including selling their possessions and given to those in need (2:45; 4:32).

It is possible to read back into New Testament texts that "breaking bread" and "table" are technical terms for celebrating the Lord's Supper, and to conclude that every time something like this term appears it describes such celebration. Scholarly opinion differs. Historically, however, such technical intepretation has not been given to these phrases. The early Christians spent plenty of time together just sharing meals, along with a lot of other things they shared. Paul's reprimand to the Corinthians in 1 Corinthians 11:20-34 is the only explicit reference to the Lord's Supper as part of their worship practice. The argument is not compelling that this special celebration happened every time the congregation came together for worship, especially since it is not mentioned in the extended discussion of worship in 1 Corinthians 14.

So, what do we know for sure happened in the congregational worship of early Christians? We recognize the ministry of the Word, including preaching and instruction; singing; praying. Both of the last two would include praise. Sometimes the Lord's Supper was celebrated.

While there is New Testament evidence of creedal statements of faith, there is no explicit reference to such in their worship. Confessions of sins and absolution may also have happened, especially as part of the ministry of the Word. But there is no explicit evidence in what the New Testament shows of their worship.

Thus we have instructive examples. Yet these fall short of prescriptions for what should be included in structured worship. This is why the Lutheran confessors regarded worship rites, ceremonies, and practices as matters of indifference about which Biblically faithful Chrsitians could differ. What is essential is presenting and responding to Christ.

III. Planning for Worship

Most discussions of worship today are really exchanges about planning for worship. There is a fundamental and very important distinction between worship and the planning for worship. One can do the latter without necessarily doing the former. Because plans for worship are not the same as authentic worship, we can and should talk about the effectiveness of various plans in various settings.

There is a distinct vocabulary for one approach to planning worship. Order, rites and ceremony (or rubric) are traditional terms used for that purpose. Order establishes ahead of time the structure--what comes before or after something else. Rite is the actual words to be spoken or sung, and the planning would involve writing the words out. Ceremony prescribes the actions to be taken; these are also called rubrics.

Ritual basically means the sum total of prescribed structure (order), words (rite), and actions (ceremony) for a worship event. Rituals are the collection of written plans, usually in a book, for various worship events, like ordinary Sunday worship, baptisms, weddings, funerals, etc.

When not meant narrowly for only the classic ritual of eucharistic celebration, liturgy is mostly used interchangeably with ritual—the prescribed detailed, written out plans for worship events.

Now it is important to realize that a plan for worship is not the same as worship. Prescribed words and actions may be done in proper order, without the relation between God and people known as worship actually happening. This is the teaching of the Lutheran Formula of Concord: "We believe teach and confess unanimously that the ceremonies and rites...are in and of themselves no divine worship or even a part of it."[9] The ceremonies referred to "are neither commanded or forbidden in the Word of God, but which have been introduced solely for the sake of good order and the general welfare." Ceremonies and rites, as the terms appear in the Latin version, add up to rituals--the plans for worship.

In relation to the high formality of traditional worship ritual, contemporary worship tends to be more informal, allowing for more spontaneity in word and action, or at least not trying to write it all out ahead of time. Yet there is still usually a plan and a well thought out one. If the plan is not the same as the event, then what should the plan try to accomplish in the event? Are some worship plans better than others for the purpose at hand? And what should those purposes be? *Questions to structure the ritual*

These are questions pastors and other worship leaders need to ask. Part of the ferment in worship practices today is growing resistance to picking up a recommended book and doing everything those plans lay out. One side—those who like the books of ritual—appreciate the assurance of richness, integrity and focus in the plans carried forward from traditions of previous centuries. The other side fears that basic outcomes are not emerging when the old plans are used. In times of ferment, the most helpful thing to do is to go back to the basics.

What does Scripture tell us should result when Christians gather to worship? Whatever we are able to identify as outcomes will enable us to determine how effective a given plan is in a given circumstance. "Effective" is not a usual word in discussion of worship, but it is necessary when pursuing the distinction between plan and event.

The next chapter will show that many of these criteria are recognized in the Formula of Concord. After identifying outcomes and conditions in what follows here, I suggest a rough ranking of them according to the planning importance of assuring their presence in the worship event. Clearly the presentation of the Word of God with its expectations and promises needs to be at the top. There may well be other criteria. I am not aware of any systematic discussions of effective worship planning that produce a delineation of criteria.

A. Outcomes Determining Effectiveness in Worship Planning

Several New Testament passages point us toward outcomes to look for. The Book to the Hebrews has the most extensive discussion of worship, showing how Jesus Christ is the fulfillment of the structured Old Testament worship. Three criteria for Christian practice emerge in chapter 10 and one more in chapter 12. Paul's first letter to the Corinthians offers two outcome statements and his letter to the Colossians clarifies two more. Jesus himself teaches a bottom-line outcome in John 4. In addition to outcome statements, Paul also states three general conditions in 1 Corinthians 14 that should be present, such as doing worship in an orderly way.

This section presents a) nine outcomes and the next one offers b) three conditions. After these are discussed, they will be put c) in an order according to how well they can be planned. Ultimately authentic worship is between God and the individual, and worship planners cannot guarantee full effectiveness for all. But planning can asses what does or does not happen and can make adjustments in the plan for a specific congregation.

In verse 22 of Hebrews 10 we are told that in Christ we can now draw near to God with sincere hearts, in full assurance of faith, and with unswerving hope in God's promises. In verse 25 the writer encourages these Christians to keep meeting together ("do not give up" meeting) and when they do, they should encourage one another. The object of that encouragement is identified in the previous verse (24): "spur one another on toward love and good deeds."

Thus worship planning is effective when those Christians assembled together: *9 things happen in worship*

- **Draw near to God with sincere hearts**. The evaluation question is whether this is happening among most worshipers. Simply telling them to do so ("Draw near with sincere hearts") has little relation to whether they actually do.

- **Find the assurance and hope of their faith.** Planning should assess whether most leave with that assurance.
- **Spur one another on toward love and good deeds.** Worship planners should be asking whether most have more of this attitude and behavior after the worship time together.

Two chapters later we are told to "worship God acceptably with reverence and awe"(Hebrews 12:28). The Greek word for reverence here appears infrequently and is different from the more common for reverence, as discussed in the first section of this chapter. It is also used in Hebrews 5: 7 for the reverent submission of Jesus when he "offered up prayer and petitions with loud cries and tears to the one who could save him from death." This emotional anxiety and fear is certainly much deeper than ceremonial decorum and propriety. The second word in 12:28, "awe," also has the root emotional sense of fear to it, as is clarified in the explanation of the following verse: "for God is a consuming fire." The basic passage undoubtedly means an emotional awareness of cautiously and prudently being in the presence of the awe-inspiring Wholly Other—God. Thus another criterion is:

- **Worship God acceptably with emotional awareness of his awesomeness.**

Two more criteria for what ought to happen in worship are found in Paul's admonitions in 1 Corinthians 14. The most explicit and general comes after the summary of content: All of what he talks about "must be done for the strengthening of the church" (14:26). The key Greek verb is *oikodomein*, and edification or strengthening are really weak translations. The basic meaning is to build together, as when the verb frequently is used to mean building the body of Christ. This is much more than edifying individuals.

A verse before this major outcome, Paul states another that is often overlooked. He states concern that an unbeliever who visits the worship of the congregation should understand what is happening and be inwardly convicted. Thus worship participants are to conduct themselves so that the visitor "will fall down and worship God, exclaiming, 'God is really among you'." (1 Corinthians 14: 25)

Thus worship planning is effective when:

- **Participants are building together the congregation as the body of Christ.**
- **A visitor is able to recognize the presence of God.**

The 14th chapter of 1 Corinthians posits the presence of instruction and hymns. For the Colossians Paul states how these components are supposed to be present: "Let the word of Christ dwell in you richly as you teach and admonish one another with all wisdom, and as you sing psalms, hymns, and spiritual songs with gratitude in your hearts to God" (Col 3:16). Thus:

- **The word of Christ should be richly present in wise teaching and admonition.**
- **Singing should be done with heart-felt gratitude.**

Finally, Jesus himself states; "God is spirit, and his worshipers must worship in spirit and in truth" (John 4: 24). The doubly used word for worship here ("worshipers," and "worship") is the one for bowing and submitting. The two terms, in spirit and in truth, are very general and have many shades of meaning in the New Testament. It is possible, though, to clarify a Lutheran understanding, since, regarding worship, the Lutheran Confessions address this passage specifically: "This passage teaches that worship should be in spirit, in faith, and with the heart."[10] The original German for this sentence states literally that such worship is "with heart, with heart-felt fear, and with heart-felt faith." With such an interpretation, the criterion for effectiveness can be stated:

- **Participants experience worship as heartfelt.**

B. Conditions for Good Worship

Several conditions ought to characterize congregational worship. These are not outcomes, but presumably worship that does not meet these criteria will have difficulty being effective.

In 1 Corinthians 14 Paul was quite concerned about avoiding confusion, "for God is not a God of disorder but of peace" (1 Cor 14: 33). Thus he urges that "everything should be done in a fitting and orderly way" (14:40). But implicit in his discussion is that there be some spontaneity, for he encourages a speaker to allow for a sudden inspiration that comes to someone sitting down (14:30). One other condition in his 1 Corinthians 14 passage is difficult to interpret. He states that women should remain silent (14:34). While 1 Timothy 2:12 clarifies his view for teaching, Lutherans have historically not interpreted this injunction to mean women should not participate in singing, praying, or confessing.

Thus, while not outcomes, clear conditions for worship include:

- **Everything should be done in a fitting and orderly way.**
- **There should be allowance for spontaneity.**

Under the special condition of eating the Lord's Supper, Paul is very strong in insisting that "whoever eats the bread and drinks the cup of the Lord" should not do so "in an unworthy manner" (1 Cor 11:27). Preparation should consist of each person examining himself or herself. What that preparation should consist of is beyond the issue at hand. The main point is the condition that:

- **Individuals should not participate in the Lord's Supper in an unworthy manner.**

Of these three conditions the one probably most controversial today concerns allowing for spontaneity in worship. Note here an observation from liturgical specialist James F. White:

> But much worship is based on spontaneity, the hardest element to study. Various types of worship contain different degrees of fixed formulas for word and action (such as are found in books) and spontaneity, which ebbs and flows as the spirit moves and is not subject to the medium of print... (Spontaneity) is nevertheless an important ingredient in contemporary (meaning current and not in contrast to traditional) worship in Western churches.
>
> Service books can only provide standard formulas. A healthy balance must remain between such formulas and the unwritten and unplanned element that only spontaneity can provide.[11]

C. Toward Assessment of Worship Planning Effectiveness

Again, the distinction between a worship plan and the actual worship event needs to be recognized. This seems commonly overlooked. The title of one of the two new Lutheran service books is significant for displaying a misunderstanding. For all of Lutheran history and for virtually all denominations today, the collection of worship materials and songs is described as a book, or hymnal or something similar. Thus the 1978 volume now in use is the *Lutheran Book of Worship*. But the 1982 version, *Lutheran Worship*, makes a rather striking presumption. The collection of materials seems equated with worship itself. Yet it is only a book that may or may not result in true worship for those who use it.

By-the-book worship planning can work well to provide for two of the three **conditions** Paul set for congregational worship. As we saw a few paragraphs ago, it does not work well for the third.

1. Everything should be done in a fitting and orderly way.
2. Individuals should be discouraged from unworthy participation in the Lord's Supper.
3. There should be allowance for spontaneity.

Further, worship planning, according to New Testament expectations, should strive for various **outcomes** among those Christians assembled together. The word "effective" applies to planning associated with these outcomes.

Effectiveness with two of the eight outcomes identified for Christians in Hebrews, 1 Corinthians, and the Gospel of John can be reasonably assured by careful scripting of the words to be said:

1. Participants find the assurance and hope of their faith.
2. They find the Word of God richly presented in wise teaching and admonition.

Two more outcomes can be verbally encouraged and even symbolically enacted through ritual but would seem better accomplished by additional provision for unscripted interaction among participants.

3. Participants spur one another on toward love and good deeds.

4. They become more built together as the body of Christ.

The remaining four outcomes are beyond direct control of the worship planners and thus have usually been left to individuals for their self evaluation and individual improvement in personal relationship with God. These have not historically been significant factors in evaluating effective of worship plans. But is this disregard wise and responsible leadership?

Two of these outcomes can be indirectly affected by leadership that pays attention to the emotional impact of how words are spoken, how music is performed and singing led, how sequence and interaction happen, and how visual surroundings are developed.

5. Singing is done with heartfelt gratitude.

6. Participants have emotional awareness of God's awesomeness.

The third of the four outcomes that touches on emotions involves the attitude of worshipers at the beginning of the worship event and thus seems other than an outcome. But surely outcomes of previous worship experiences will influence attitudes brought to the one at hand.

7. Participants draw near to God with sincere hearts.

The final outcome is more or less the bottom line

8. Participants' worship is heartfelt and in spirit as well as in truth.

Ultimately no person can determine the quality of the worship experience of another. This is between God and that person. And Lutherans believe God initiates that relationship and develops its quality. Thus the means by which God works his grace through Word and sacraments have to be fundamental to worship planning.

The strength of the way the objective Word and sacrament are featured in a service that follows the classic communion liturgy was underscored for me at the end of a recent weekend renewal retreat for which I was pastor. There had been much sharing of subjective spiritual experiences by participants. Some of their personal stories were very moving and helpful to others. Then to say and sing together the certainty of God's promises as presented in Divine Service

II, and then to receive the assurance of the sacrament was a fitting and powerful close that pulled the whole weekend together.

What about the times when worship leaders have provided Word and sacraments and a significant percentage of participants say they have not experienced heartfelt worship or react that way without describing their disappointment, or no longer even expect to be engaged in spirit as well as in truth? Should pastors worry? The easy answer is No; its the fault of the individuals who need to learn how to appreciate the rich feast to which they are invited. But surely that is too easy an answer, especially when there is the possibility that different planning or better preparation might yield a different outcome. Surely worship planners ought constantly to be asking how better leadership in all aspects of the service might be associated with greater effectiveness in stimulating worship "in spirit and in truth."

The Apostle Paul presents one more outcome that dare not be overlooked in worship planning faithful to Scriptural expectations.

9. A visitor should be able to recognize the presence of God.

Obviously the answer to whether that happens lies with the visitor. Asking visitors as well as current participants what their experience was like would seem a basic part of good worship planning. How often does that happen?

Such pragmatism is not part of the accepted tradition, and leaders of the liturgical renewal movement of the last several decades were not at all inclined to listen to those they would lead in worship. With regret, one of those leaders, Gracia Grindal, cites the outrage of many participants in a 1991 Hymn Society meeting at a speaker's suggestion that, instead of looking for answers about how to invigorate worship and music in the libraries, they should develop systematic ways of asking the people in the pews and choir lofts what they thought and felt about it. Those who resisted assumed that such people have no wisdom to share on the issue.[12]

But the New Testament worship leaders were not afraid to be pragmatic. They were willing to identify standards for the worship they sought. Those criteria beg the question of effectiveness—was the actual worship associated with those outcomes? The Apostle Paul was not content to rest on tradition but was willing to make judgments on what was happening to the worshipers. Isn't that still the way to approach effectiveness in worship today?

[1] W. Nicholls, *Jacob's Ladder: The Meaning of Worship*, Ecumenical Studies in Worship No. 4, London: Lutterworth, 1958, p. 9.

[2] Don McMinn, *The Practice of Praise*, Word Music, 1992, p. 41.

[3] Ibid., p. 67.

[4] David Peterson, *Engaging With God: A Biblical Theology of Worship*,Eerdmans, 1992, p. 73.

[5] Ibid., p. 72.

[6] Ibid., p. 72.

[7] H. Strathman, "leitourgeo," *Theological Dictionary of the New Testament*, ed Gerhard Kittel and Gerhard Friedrich, translated and abridged by Geoffrey W. Bromiley, Eerdmans, 1985, p. 528

[8] James F. White, *Introduction to Christian Worship*, Abingdon, 1980, p. 24.

[9] "Epitome to the Formula of Concord," Article X, *The Book of Concord*, trans and ed. by Theodore G. Tappert, Muhlenberg Press, 1959, p. 493.

[10] "Apology to the Augsburg Confession, Article 24, op.cit., 254.

[11] James F. White, *Introduction to Christian Worship*, Abingdon Press, 1980, pp. 30,31.

[12] Gracia Grindal, "Faithful in the Face of Change," *Word and World*, Vol XII, No 3 (Summer 1992), p. 225.

Chapter 5

What Is Lutheran Worship?

"That's not Lutheran!"

This reaction is common among those who first experience contemporary worship in a Lutheran church. I recall a family visiting our Sunday service. In discussion before the service, the father explained that they had moved back into the area. His wife still liked the old hymnal, but, announced with a certain tinge of pride, he now preferred the new. He did not know what to make out of my explanation that we did not use any hymnal but had a very simple service. They did not return. We did not fit within their experience of Lutheran, even though we feature a very clear statement of distinctive Lutheran emphases in our beliefs. I am sure they told others, "They're not Lutheran."

The accusation that something is not Lutheran is important to hear and should be taken very seriously. In this particular case, it meant losing a potential family with a strong church background. But that is a calculated risk when moving beyond well-known tradition. The reason for wanting to do so emerges from the basic mission for a specific congregation. But we get ahead of ourselves.

How does one determine whether something is Lutheran? Do you visit dozens or hundreds of congregations to see what they are doing (an exercise that would undoubtedly produce surprises)? Is the common denominator among them what you are looking for? Do you put something to vote among official delegates at a convention and let the majority at that time and place rule? How far over the land and across the years do you look?

One of the distinctions of being Lutheran Christians is that we have a ready-made, time-tested way to answer the question, What is Lutheran? To be Lutheran is to subscribe to the Confessions of the Evangelical Lutheran Church, as formulated in the century of the Reformation that gave birth to Protestantism. This is the official common denominator linking all churches calling themselves Lu-

60

theran together into the largest Protestant grouping of any Christian church body in the world.

But the Confessions are not really the starting point. They declare themselves to be only an interpretation of the real starting point, Scripture. In the sixteenth-century conflicts over truth and church practices, confessors took positions only on what they could defend on the basis of Scripture. If Scripture did not take a position—if something was neither commanded nor forbidden by God in his Word—they said so and left the matter open for differences in practice.

I. The Basic Principle for a Lutheran Understanding of Worship: Local Authority to Plan

The public Sunday worship of a congregation is one of those areas they left open. It is tempting to say they took no position, but that would be an understatement. In the Formula of Concord, the confessors went out of their way to state very forcefully that there was no single mandated form or pattern for public worship. "We believe, teach and confess" are the strongest words they could use to state a principle. Here is that fundamental principle for a Lutheran understanding of church worship:

> We further believe, teach, and confess that the community of God in every place and at every time has the right, authority, and power to change, to reduce, or to increase ceremonies according to its circumstances, as long as it does so without frivolity and offense but in an orderly and appropriate way, as at any time may seem to be most profitable, beneficial, and salutary for good order, Christian discipline, evangelical decorum, and the edification of the church. Paul instructs us how we can with a good conscience give in and yield to the weak in faith in such external matters of indifference. (underlining added) (Formula of Concord, Solid Declaration Article X on Church Usages, paragraph 9[1])

This statement has three components to be highlighted.

1. The subject is "ceremonies."

Other sentences in this section talk about "ceremonies and church rites." These terms are used advisedly and mean specifically the actions and words that are written ahead of time for what is to be done in a public worship service.

The confessors could have said, Each congregation may worship as it chooses. This is basically what they meant. But they knew the plan (ceremonies and rites) is not the same as true worship. Several paragraphs earlier in the condensed version of the Formula of Concord, the Epitome, they teach and confess that ceremonies and rites "are in and of themselves no divine worship or even part of it."[2] They did not presume to equate planning for worship and worship itself. Such constraint among advocates of differing worship plans today would be in order, too. This especially needs to be said to those prone to equate printed liturgies and worship.

2. The confessors stated criteria by which worship practices should be evaluated.

Whatever ceremonies are chosen, they need to be justified according to whether they are "profitable, beneficial, and salutary." Changes should furthermore be made in an orderly and appropriate way without frivolity and offense.

For someone to declare personal preference is not enough. Nor is it sufficient planning simply to copy what was done in other cultures and times. The basic issue is whether a practice is productive for the congregation that would adopt it. And there is no doubt but that the reference is to a specific congregation ("the community of God in every place and at every time") and not to the church in general, or even a synod or denomination.

The standards by which to judge benefit are:

- good order
- Christian discipline   (training in piety, in the Latin)
- evangelical decorum   (Gospel-based fear of God, in a German explanation)
- edification of the church

The Christian discipline refers to teaching and training, as indicated in the Latin. Evangelical decorum is much more than propriety; one of the earliest footnoted comments explains this as doing everything with a sense of seriousness and honor so that people can experience the fear of God, the awesomeness of God. Edification of the church means its upbuilding, or building it together.

Instructive is comparing these confessional criteria to those found in Scripture, as presented in the previous chapter. Scriptural writers expected that those who gather for worship:

- Find the Word of God richly presented (Formula of Concord: Christian teaching and training),
- Be drawn near to God with gratitude, awe, and submission (FC: Gospel-based fear of God),
- Be built together as the body of Christ (FC: edification of the church),
- Encourage one another in their Christian living (FC: edification of the church as well as Christian teaching and training.)

Missing from this confessional list is a concern for visitors. But missing from the Lutheran confessions in general is a concern for evangelism or outreach to those not in the folds of the church. At its beginning Lutheranism was a movement to reform the existing church, not to extend it. In those yet Medieval times, the church was still seen as including virtually all members of their explicitly Christian society and political units. Facing the pressing problems of their time and society, the concern of the confessors for how to bring the message to those who did not consider themselves Christians was not nearly as high on their agenda for the Reformation as it was for the Apostle Paul, for instance.

The caution of Article X against frivolity and offense when making changes in worship practices is always appropriate, as is Paul's principle that worship should be done in a fitting and orderly way. The judgment of what is frivolous and offensive, however, remains with the responsible leadership of the congregation considering the changes, as noted next in the third point highlighted in this principle. If worship leaders cannot convince a church's designated leaders that proposed changes are reasonable, then the changes would probably not be fruitful anyhow. The possibility of making changes in only one of several available services often reduces the risk of serious offense.

3. The confessors recognized the authority of an individual congregation to arrange its own practices ("ceremonies") as it sees fit for its circumstances.

This is the basic point of this paragraph of the Formula of Concord. The year was 1580—50 years after the Augsburg Confession (the first major one) and 63 years after the beginning of the Reformation. By that time the movement had spread and established itself in many jurisdictions of what had become Protestant Northern Europe. There already was diversity of worship among the Lutherans, as there has been ever since. By that time, as the statement of the issue implies, there were already some ceremonies that had fallen into disuse.

Would the confessors have recognized the need "to change, reduce, or increase ceremonies" for the purpose of reaching out to the unchurched? Read on to understand the explanation to Martin Luther's own preference when it came to choosing specific "ceremonies."

II. Changes In Worship Practices Should Meet the Needs of Those Who Would Worship

The definitive statement on local autonomy in worship practices appeared in the final confession of 1580, the Formula of Concord, when extensive diversity was already a fact. A seemingly different position is stated in the first, the Augsburg Confession of 1530.

> Our churches are falsely accused of abolishing the Mass. Actually, the Mass is retained among us and is celebrated with the greatest reverence. Almost all the customary ceremonies are also retained, except that German hymns are interspersed here and there among the parts sung in Latin. (Augsburg Confession, Article XXIV on The Mass, paragraph 1[3])

Conservatives argue you can't use evangelical stuff because its theological underpinnings can't be ignored. You can't baptize it Lutheran. However, if the Catholic mass isn't filled w/ theological presuppositions which stem from a Catholic theology, I don't know what is! Yet Luther said "keep it". He baptized it Lutheran!

In 1530 the Reformation was still new and fighting for its political right to exist. Above all, the movement was about theology and the centrality of justification by grace through faith. As established in disputes with radicals, the Reformation was not about abolishing external, familiar forms of practice. An emphasis on externalities would detract from the core focus on grace and the freedom it brings. Thus there was a clear preference to retain as much of customary practices as could be rightfully used.

One reason for restraint was political. Why pick fights where unnecessary? Thus the article which begins with the statement on retaining the Mass closes, in essence, with the summary appeal: Since we have made no conspicuous changes in the public ceremonies of the mass, it is unfair to criticize our worship as heretical or unchristian.

But there was also a more substantive underlying reason for this conservatism in public worship. The Mass, the classic liturgical order of service culminating in the Lord's Supper, was the most common form of worship at that time. It is what everyone—Luther, other leaders and the ordinary people—knew best. Respect for their need for continuity and familiarity, especially at a time of so much upheaval, led to retention of as much of the traditional worship as was theologically acceptable.

Some interpreters would say that retention of the basic Mass was done out of recognition of its inherent superiority as a worship form. Thus Lutheran liturgical scholar Luther Reed assumes that all regarded it "as a perfect and finished product."[4] But no evidence is cited.

In contrast, Luther scholar Vilmos Vajta bases the reason for retention on respect for familiarity. He says, "It is this love for his fellow-men that prompted Luther's conservative approach to the question of liturgical form."[5] Public worship needs order and form. There is no harm in traditional liturgical forms used properly. So the principle was to use what they know. Reed himself notes that Luther "recognized the fact that the whole devotional and ceremonial system of the church was deeply impressed upon popular imagination."

Based on extensive quotes from Luther, Vajta goes on to formulate this principles for Luther's understanding of public worship:

"The choice of forms is however not a matter of personal preference, but must depend on the need of our fellows. The liturgical choice of the 'outer man,' his decision for or against certain forms should be dictated by the need of others."[6]

Drawing on various statements by Luther, Vajta goes on to explain Luther's perspective:

> (The common people) clung to the traditional liturgical forms as tenaciously as the pope, but for different reasons. The ceremoniacs were smug and stubborn. But the people were conservative only because they were weak in faith. Christian love demanded greater patience with them than with the self-righteous papists. After centuries of papist perversion, the people could not be expected to embrace the freedom of faith in a flash. Luther was well aware of this fact, and all his liturgical reforms betray his concern for the spiritual well-being of the weak in faith.[7]

"Lest the common people get confused and discouraged" is a phrase expressing this focus on needs of the weak. Luther used it in a letter appealing to church leaders in Dorpat, Livonia (now in Estonia) to strive for a uniform practice of worship in their district. The year was 1525, a time of great civil unrest. The occasion was upheaval in this city caused by a self-proclaimed Luther disciple who was urging the rejection of traditional worship and the destruction of paintings and statues in the churches of that city.

In his letter Luther wrote that since quarreling over external rites and order is confusing to common people, the leaders should get together in a friendly manner and come to a decision they can agree on concerning these external matters, which in and of themselves are not important. He points them toward two desired outcomes: so there be uniform practice instead of disorder and so that the common people not get confused and discouraged.[8]

Sometimes in the worship debates of today, Luther's Livonian appeal is used to urge uniformity on a whole synod as a properly Lutheran thing to do. But uniformity among the handful of churches governed by the city council of this small town was not his main point. Luther's driving concern was to avoid confusion and discouragement among the weak. The main point of that letter is for leaders to exercise wisdom in putting aside personal preferences and fashioning agreements about worship practices that could be understood and appreciated by ordinary Christians. This is still essential advice for any church governing body today. That uniformity is not the main point was clarified 55 years alter in the Formula of Concord, as noted shortly.

III. It Is Essential To Avoid Liturgical Legalism

From their experience in the 50 years after the Augsburg Confession, the confessors in the Formula of Concord formulated six basic principles about what needs to be avoided in matters of "Ecclesiastical Rites That Are Called Adiaphora or Things Indifferent" (Formula of Concord, Solid Declaration, Article 10). Principle 5 states:

> 5. We also reject and condemn the procedure whereby matters of indifference are abolished in such a way as to give the impression that the community of God does not have the liberty to use one or more ceremonies at any time and place, according to its circumstances, as may in Christian liberty be most beneficial to the church.[9]

At issue is the theologically necessary avoidance of any form of legalism in our relationship with God. Defense of Christian liberty is at the heart of justification by grace through faith. Several paragraphs earlier, here is where the Formula of Concord stands on the issue of forcing worship practices as necessary:

> As soon as this article (on Christian liberty) is weakened and human commandments are forcibly imposed on the church as necessary and as though their omission were wrong or sinful, the door has been opened to idolatry, and ultimately the commandments of men will be increased and be put as divine worship not only on par with God's commandments, but even above them.[10]

Christian liberty, by the way, applies to the freedom to use any form, as well as to resist such use. Thus Luther also strongly opposed the radicals in the Reformation who condemned every ecclesiastical tradition that could not be traced directly to the Bible. Vajta observes:

> Luther meant to follow a middle road between them and the papists. He felt free to borrow from the right or the left, for his picture of evangelical freedom lifted him far above the liturgical factions. The sectarianism of liturgical legalists was an offense to him, for while the law will cause divisions, the gospel should bring about unity.[11]

IV. Unity in Doctrine Is Not Disrupted By Diversity in Worship Practices

The point about relying on the Gospel to bring about unity leads to the basic principle about worship practices most relevant to issues today. The bottom line is Principle 6 in Article X of the Formula of Concord. It immediately follows Principle 5 about avoiding the impression that churches do not have liberty in choices of ceremonies. Principle 6 explains:

> 6. In line with the above, churches will not condemn each other because of a difference in ceremonies, when in Christian liberty one uses fewer or more of them, as long as they are otherwise agreed in doctrine and in all its articles and the right use of the holy sacraments, according to the well-known axiom, "Disagreement in fasting should not destroy agreement in faith."[12]

Discussions among Lutherans about worship in the 1990's sometimes take on the tone of a struggle for the soul of Lutheranism. Such is often the view of those who see contemporary or alternative worship as a threat to what they see reclaimed as "true" Lutheran worship. This perspective simply does not fit with the basic principles of the Lutheran Confessions. The soul of Lutheranism is justification by grace through faith and the necessary avoidance of legalism. Art Just !

V. Attentiveness To The Weak in Faith Should Drive Both Change And Conformity in Worship Practices.

If love, especially for the weak in faith, was the driving force in Luther's thoughts about worship practices, as Vajta demonstrates, then that love can lead in two seemingly contradictory directions.

One direction is to prevent confusion by maintaining good order through uniformity among churches where appropriate. According to Vajta, Luther's "principle of love and regard for the common man made him the sworn enemy of arbitrary changes."[13]

Yet such uniformity could not be simplistically applied. Thus Luther, according to Vajta, also thought that "the order of love precluded liturgical uniformity." Luther's main rationale for this position is that diversity might keep people from assigning too much importance to the form of the service. Recognizing the diverse needs of people, he even went further and made the eye-popping claim that love will call for many changes, even as a tree sprouts new blooms and fruits every year.[14]

So, what is it? Should Lutherans strive for uniformity in worship practices? Or should they be ready to make changes, even frequent ones, for good reason? As is so often the case in Lutheran understandings, the answer is Yes—Yes to both. Uniformity and change each has its place. Wisdom is needed to understand their relationship.

Near the beginning of Article X the Formula of Concord confessors formulate one approach to the tension by using the Apostle Paul's position on Jewish religious observances, especially circumcision, among early Christians. These really were matters of indifference. Yet one time he could insist on circumcision (Acts 16:3), but when freedom in the Gospel was at stake by some who insisted on circumcision, "we did not give in to them for a moment" (Gal 2:5). Paul gave in to the weak as far as foods, times, and days were concerned (Romans 14:5,6). Yet resisting "human traditions" he would not yield to those who would pass judgment on what Christians eat or drink, or with regard to a festival or a new moon or a sabbath (Col 2:16).[15]

Applying this principle to worship practices, we can say that giving in to the weak in matters of uniformity and consistency in Sunday services is generally a good thing and even a loving thing to do. But as soon as someone insists that uniformity is necessary in order to be a good Lutheran, then this stance must be resisted for the sake of the centrality in Lutheran theology of freedom in the Gospel. Put in even more practical terms, the day some decision-making body assumes authority to insist that only one form of worship is acceptable to be faithful Lutherans is the day those faithful to the Lutheran confessions need to resist and pursue alternate forms of worship.

Thus regarding agreed-upon worship practices, Luther could urge that "a preacher must watch and diligently instruct the people lest they take such uniform practices as divinely appointed and absolutely binding laws."[16]

The principle of love for the weak can and should be carried a step further. Those already in the church whose weakness is dependence on familiar tradition are not the only weak in the faith. Following the confessors' approach of looking for Scriptural analogies (although this one they did not offer), we can learn from the apostles' approach to new Christian in Acts 15. The issue again was circumcision as a religious observance. The council which was convened to settle the sharp dispute about its necessity among Gentiles concluded that uniformity in this Jewish practice was not necessary to be a Christian. The rationale was not just preserving freedom in the Gospel. Here it was the love-motivated desire that "we should not make it difficult for the Gentiles who are turning to God" (Acts 15:19).

What about the unchurched today who are turning to God and are ready to come to church? Many find the highly developed and even complicated ritual of current service settings in Lutheran worship books to be a burden on their way to being drawn to God. Thus wisdom in finding the way between uniformity and change would leave room for congregations and their leaders who decide they will not make it difficult for the unchurched and will develop simpler, more accessible, more "user-friendly" forms of worship.

In most cases, congregations do not have to make a decision about which weakness should drive their worship planning—the weakness of those dependent on familiar tradition or the weakness of those who find the tradition a barrier. Two different services can be offered. It is hard to imagine an established Lutheran congregation completely moving away from the formats of the *Lutheran Book of Worship*, or *Lutheran Worship*, or *The Lutheran Hymnal*. That would be an unloving and even cruel thing to do to members who use these formats well for their worship. But it would also be unloving for the established worshipers to insist theirs is the only proper Lutheran worship and to deny well-reasoned alternatives for reaching out to those who do not share the tradition. planned

Footnote: The Lutheran Confessions Do Not Talk About "The Liturgy."

Much of the discussion of Lutheran worship today carries and even features the term "liturgy" and "the liturgy." I do not recall growing up as a Lutheran and even attending seminary that I heard the same allegiance to the term. While re-reading references to worship in the Lutheran Confessions for this project, I kept note of occurrences of the term "liturgy." It shows up in one section of the Apology of the Augsburg Confession.[17] In other parts there are two passing references in the English translation where "liturgy" does not appear in the original Latin or German.

The Apology of the Augsburg Confession is two and a half times longer than the Augsburg Confession which it defends. After the first confession was made to the Emperor at the Diet of Augsburg in June, 1530, Emperor Charles V asked for a response from the Roman party. This "Roman Confutation" was presented in August. In response to that, the "Apology" at length defended and explained the first formulation.

The section in the Apology is instructive. The issue at hand in the relevant section of the predecessor Augsburg Confession was whether the mass form of worship, by definition of that term, has to be a sacrifice, which the Roman Confutation claimed and a position which the followers of Luther stoutly resisted. Expunging the sacrificial understanding is the main point of Article XXIV.

In refuting the Augsburg Confession, the opponents claimed the term "liturgy" was used by the Greeks to mean sacrifice. In responding, the apologists explained their understanding of liturgy. They, logically, were at pains to disassociate the term from sacrifice. What is one sentence in the original German is expanded in the Latin in what could be called a footnote, introduced by the sentence, "But let us talk about the term 'liturgy'." They point out that philologists (a linguistic discipline freshly emerging in the Renaissance) derive it not from a root word that means prayer but from a root that means public goods or public service. While rightfully understood, the word can be applied to worship ceremonies (for the public service of showing forth the body and blood to the people), the apologists' main point is that the term "liturgy" basically means ministry or service done as a public duty. Their examples of the right use, from ancient literature and Pauline writings, are not worship ceremonies. Thus while "liturgy" could be used in reference to worship ceremonies, the apologists preferred not to do so.

Conclusions

If the concern of church leaders today is to be authentically Lutheran according to the Lutheran Confessions, then these positions and behaviors should be followed:

1. Stop insisting there is only one proper form of Lutheran worship. There can be no room for liturgical legalism among Lutherans.

2. Recognize the rights of individual Lutheran congregations to chose worship practices that best fit their circumstances and mission. Diversity in worship practices in itself does not disrupt unity in doctrine.

3. Do not condemn other churches and pastors because of differences in worship forms.

4. In addition, if Luther's approach to worship forms is to be respected, then let love be the motivating factor in planning worship and deciding among alternative forms. This should be love for the weak in faith, which includes but is not limited only to those who want the familiarity of traditional forms.

5. Stop talking about "the liturgy." This is not confessional language. General use of "liturgy" is not even historically Lutheran until this century. The proper confessional terms are ceremonies, rites or church practices.

---

[1] 1. *Book of Concord*, trans. and ed. by Theodore G. Tappert, Muhlenberg Press, p. 612. The original languages in *Die Bekenntnisschriften der evangelisch-lutherischen Kirche*, 4th edition, Goetteingen: Vandnehoeck and Ruprecht, 1959, p. 1056.

[2] Tappert, op. cit., p. 494.

[3] Ibid., p. 56.

[4] Luther D. Reed, *The Lutheran Liturgy*, Muhlenberg Press, 1959, p. 71.

[5] Vilmos Vajta, *Luther On Worship: An Interpretation*, Mughlenberg Press, 1958, p. 174.

[6] Ibid., p. 177.

[7] Ibid., p. 179, 180.

[8] Martin Luther, . "A Christian Exhortation to the Livonians Concerning Public Worship and Concord, 1525," in *Luther's Works, Volume 53: Liturgy and Hymns*, edited by Ulrich S. Leupold, Fortress Press, 1965, pp 42-50.

[9] Tappert, op. cit., p. 615.

[10] Ibid., p. 615.

[11] Vajta, op. cit., p. 179.

[12] Tappert, op. cit., p. 616.

[13] Vajta, op. cit., p. 183

[14] Ibid., p. 177.

[15] Ibid., p. 612.

[16] Luther, "A Christian Exhortation to the Livonians," op. cit., p. 48.

[17] Tappert, op. cit., p. 264.`

Chapter 6

How Representative of Lutheranism Is Today's Dominant Worship Style?

If contemporary worship does not strike many as Lutheran worship, what is?

Ask almost any middle-aged Lutheran today and you will wind up focusing on what is presented in current service books. That's understandable. But is this easy reference sufficient to give a definitive answer? In a time of increasing experimentation with alternatives, do the currently endorsed books have the necessary weight to settle the issue?

The way the question is phrased invites attention to history. In fact, the worship plans presented in current service books do not represent the way most Lutherans have worshiped in most of Lutheran history. Old-timers who grew up in many different parts of this country in the early part of this century can witness to the fact of change.

 As noted in the previous chapter, the confessions that define Lutheran make a special point of allowing diversity in worship practices, along with expecting good reasons for changes. Since the confessors refrained from being definitive, where else can we look for an authoritative answer to what Lutheran worship is than to how Lutherans have actually worshiped over time?

The only alternative to generalizations from history is to insist on the form that has emerged as dominant today. The average Lutheran-in-the-pew can be excused for doing that. But responsible church leaders who want to be authentically Lutheran cannot. Unlike theological issues, worship issues cannot be brought into uniformity by political insistence on turning worship forms into the equivalent of orthodoxy.

Raw political power in this or that jurisdiction may try to do so and may even prevail in a vote. But then any claim of faithfulness to the defining Lutheran Confessions has been forfeited.

The history of Lutheran worship can be told two ways. These are two perspectives that yield two different stories.

The currently more popular story is about the successful, decades-long, even century-long struggle to restore Lutheran worship from a corrupted state to its original glory. The current service books essentially culminate that process. This is the Restoration Story.

The Other Story is of congregations and various Lutheran church bodies adapting their worship practices to the circumstances they faced and to the mission they chose. In point of fact, the creative part of this story covers many more years. These years span the time that saw Lutheranism's growth into the largest Protestant church body in the world.

One sub-theme in these stories is the cycling between unity and diversity. Another is perceptions of the differences in the recipients for whom this planning was done. Each story has its heroes--and its villains, Both are important to hear for those who want to be Lutheran today.

That a church body has two versions of its history is not surprising. This can reflect a diversity of mission and emphases that comes from being a large body with a long history and a rich mixture of God-given interests and giftedness among its people. Familiarity with the full history can best equip leaders of today to deal constructively and creatively with the ministry challenges of our times.

The Restoration Story

The leading hero for the Restoration Story in America is Luther D. Reed. His is also the easiest version of the story to tell because he has "written the book" on the subject. He lived and worked in the first part of this century. His defining book is *The Lutheran Liturgy*, first published in 1947 and revised in 1959. It has long been the basic textbook for worship classes in Lutheran seminaries.

For Reed, the two most important dates in his story are 1523 and 1958, with 1888 an important milestone. In this version, the 435

years in between were about how, "a church which had been confused in its thinking, unfamiliar with its own history, uncertain of its
objectives, and weak in its organization was brought to self-respect
and united endeavor."[1]

The Beginning

The year 1523 is important because Luther then published his
"Formula Missae", sometimes translated as "Formula of the Mass
and Communion." Significantly, its full title is "An Order of Mass
and Communion for the Church at Wittenberg." Reed call this "his
greatest liturgical writing." Earlier that year confusion had reigned
at the parish church in Wittenberg, which, with its University, was
the home and center of the Reformation. Luther's colleague, the
University provost Andreas Karlstadt, was leading radical efforts to
remove all vestiges of Roman Catholicism from church life, including
art and liturgical forms, in order to return to more basic spiritual life
and worship. Preaching an approach of moderation and conservative
reform, Luther prepared a form of the Latin Service. It has essentially the same order and progression as found in the most recent divine services of the current Lutheran books of worship.

The two stories present a different rationale for the order of
service that emerged. Dealing with widespread confusion is common
to both. The Restoration Story sees the choice for a purified form of
the historical mass motivated by appreciation "for the fact that the
Mass was everywhere regarded as a supreme form of devotion perfected by centuries of thought and enhanced by all the resources of
art."[2] The Other Story, as you will see, identifies the motivation as
concern for the weak in faith who knew only this type of worship.

In any event, by the time of the Augsburg Confession in 1530 the
Reformers could make the conservative and politically helpful claim
that the Mass is retained. The changes made revolved around expunging references to the eucharist as a sacrifice. The various sensi-
tivities and corrections are explained in the 20 pages devoted to the
Mass in Article XXIV of the Apology of the Augsburg Confession.

The Long Slide into Degeneracy

According to the Restoration Story it was unfortunate for the cause that Luther allowed degeneration to happen already in 1526 when he published his "German Mass and Order of Service." It is a considerably simplified form. Again, interpretations of rationale differ. In the Restoration Story, he "was practically forced to prepare a German service."[3] Also, he did not approve of what others were doing in the vernacular and he distrusted the spirit which produced hasty and immature forms.

In Luther's time and almost up to the 20th century, Germany was really a collection of independent states and cities which in effect became independent districts of a larger entity, Lutheranism, that existed only in name and common confession but was never organizationally centralized. Each district developed its own church order for organization and regulation, including directions for worship. By 1555 there were 135 church orders. Almost all based their worship on the simplified German Mass. As the Restoration Story goes, "In doing this they failed to appreciate Luther's own view of the German Mass as intended only for the uneducated laity.... They perpetuated an abnormal and temporary situation.... These districts dropped to the level of the simplest and easiest form of vernacular worship and stayed there."[4] Consequently, despite impressive solidarity in doctrinal formulation, for many centuries Lutheranism "in the spheres of worship and practical church life has been provincial."[5]

The situation only got worse in the 17th, 18th, and most of the 19th century, according to this perspective. Beyond question, the ravages of the 30 Years War (1618-1648) practically destroyed Germany and most of its culture. The German population was reduced from 16,000,000 to less than 6,000,000. In the War's wake stepped two of the four culprits seen as causing continued degeneration of worship as it should be. The first was Orthodoxy, followed by Pietism, and these led in the 18th century to Rationalism. All along from the beginning there has been the general culprit of "Reformed tendencies."

Orthodoxy was the first reaction to chaos. Its goal of restoring orderly church life placed great emphasis on achieving and enforcing precise definitions of belief and detailed prescriptions for worship.

The church became more of a department of government, with attendance required and often imposition of fines for absence. Thus, "clerical scholasticism and governmental bureaucracy reduced church life and worship to mechanical levels."[6] Worship was externalized. (One may wonder whether these are still valid concerns with orthodoxies today.)

The general reaction was given the name Pietism. It was a movement to return to spiritual basics and to awakening or reviving the church from coldness and institutionalism. Some of its emphases were focus on the clergy, insisting on a personal Christian character of those who hold the office and on expecting more effective and applied preaching. Much of the emphasis was on general involvement of laity in Bible reading, personal devotion, and prayer; small groups for Bible study and prayer frequently appeared.

The impact on public worship was that the "liturgical and formal in liturgical worship gave way to expressions of individual ideas and emotions." Formality gave way to informality in worship practices and especially in prayers. "Pietism with its intensely personal limitations neither understood nor long used what remained of the restrained and polished forms of the church's historical liturgical system."[7] (One may observe that worship is receiving increased attention as an issue today largely because many worship leaders are learning to see informaility as a strength rather than a weakness.)

Rationalism began taking over in the mid-18th century as the European Age of Enlightenment put human reason as the foundation of authority. The philosophical movement of Rationalism had a huge impact on the educated leadership elite of Germany as well as most of Europe. It was essentially the roots of what is labeled "secular humanism" today. An ideal of happiness was substituted for the divine plan of redemption. Practical interests rather than orthodox doctrines or high spirituality were stressed in the pulpit. The impact of Rationalism on worship was wholly destructive. In Reed's account, "Pietism had rejected or neglected many of the ancient forms but had not denied their content. Rationalism rejected content and form alike."[8] (One may wonder whether Rationalism's current descendant, Liberalism, is reacting the opposite way by emphasizing form to compensate for weakened content.)

The fourth culprit in the story of the decline of Lutheran worship was "Reformed tendencies." These go back to the worship practices developed by Ulrich Zwingli and John Calvin in the early years of the Reformation. They saw themselves breaking with the historical church and attempting a revival of worship as it was done in the early church. According to Reed, "they ran counter, however, to primitive practice in subordinating eucharistic worship to a new type of service which consisted chiefly of preaching, exhortation, psalm-singing and prayer.... They made of it a subjective exercise which stressed fellowship, prayer, exhortation, and instruction, and which centered chiefly on preaching and other personal activities (prayers, etc.) by the minister."[9] *Now, isn't that horrible?! (sarcasm finished now!)*

Several subplots or side movements come in the form of more "isms" to add to the "scholasticism, state control, subjectivism, intellectualism, and undue influence of Calvin"[10] and should be included among the culprits that kept a universal Christian tradition lost among Lutherans in America. These are primitivism and ethnicism.

Primitivism has to to with the pioneer conditions in America through much of the 19th century. This problem resolved itself through the American success story of social progress, especially in upgrading educational attainments. The dramatic increase in the college-educated, middle and professional class in Lutheran churches after the Second World War presented a rich field and even a demand for upgraded worship. This cultural shift can be seen as the driving force behind ready acceptance of the Restoration Story. The cultural implications of this effort deserves a whole later chapter to itself.

Ethnicism recognizes the great diversity of language and cultures among the Lutherans that landed in this country. In addition to the many sometimes quite different versions of German traditions, these included Danish, Swedish, Norwegian, Finish, Estonian, and Slovakian. In the Restorationists' view, there could be no progress towards unity as long as such diversity prevailed.

The solution to the language problem presented itself over time through assimilation into the American melting pot, aided to no small degree by the First World War. The solution to developing a common English language service presented itself through the leadership of the Lutherans who had been in America the longest and were the earliest assimilated. These were on the East Coast, especially in the Pennsylvania Ministerium. Chief among them in this century was Luther Reed, who taught and was then president at Luther Theological Seminary in Philadelphia from 1910-45. As the ethnics, primarily in the mid-West, looked about for an English version of their Lutheran worship, they were easily attracted to the one that had been around the longest in this country. Thus the East Coast Common Service of 1888 had widening acceptance over succeeding decades.

But when the ethnics looked for a service in English, they picked up more than just another language. This was because the worship leaders taking the lead back East in the latter part of the 19th-century happened to be strongly influenced by the concurrent University-led Oxford Renewal Movement movement in England that had only indirect relation to Lutheranism.

To wrap up this degeneration phase of the Restoration Story, we need to recognize what the heroes of this story were facing: "The revival of faith and church life here (in America), as in Europe, has had to make its way against powerful odds. Had these destructive forces not been so strong, so pervasive, and so long continued, the church would be further along in the recovery of its ancient heritage in worship, church music, and liturgical art of every kind."[11]

Restoration Triumphant

Now, on with the restoration.

The story is told from the perspective of Lutheranism in America. Thus 1888 is the important milestone of completion of the Common Service by cooperative work of a joint committee of the United Synod, General Synod and United Synod South. With minor modifications, this formulation of the worship service was published in the service book of each synod. It was partial realization of the ideal of a "Common Service Book for all English Speaking Lutherans."[12]

That ideal was first enunciated by Henry Melchior Muhlenberg, who is generally regarded as the major 18th-century leader of Lutheranism in America. Shortly before his death in 1778 he wrote, "It would be a most delightful and advantageous thing if all Evangelical Lutheran congregations in North America were united into one another, if they all used the same order of service."[13] This proved to be a very powerful dream that energized two centuries of consensus building, cooperation and mergers that culminated in the final merger yielding the Evangelical Lutheran Church in America in 1988.

But we get ahead of development of the Restoration.

The mid-19th century saw something summarized as the Oxford movement occur in the Church of England. Much of Protestantism in England had by then gone off into Wesleyanism and Evangelicalism. What was left of the Church of England had become spiritually destitute and subject to manipulations of secular politics. The call for reform from "national apostasy" originated and was led by churchmen at the University of Oxford. Far from the populist movement of Evangelicalism, they developed a state-funded, University-led movement. They placed considerable emphasis on revival of church life through recovered liturgical forms and got caught up in rediscovering Medievalism as part of the Romanticism prevalent at the time. Appreciation for Roman Catholicism grew, and this direction of interest was made evident in the conversion of many Oxford movement leaders, especially John Henry Newman, to Roman Catholic priesthood.

In Luther Reed's Restoration Story, the committee of the Pennsylvania ministerium who prepared the very first English language service in 1866 "availed itself of the latest developments in England."[14] While there was renewed interest in liturgical matters in Germany in the 19th century, this was mostly under Roman Catholic leadership. In one description those committee members "imbibed the Anglo-Catholic revival of their time... They began a tradition of revising and restoring, along with their teachers and counterparts in the Anglican tradition."[15]

Specialists from the liturgical renewal movement can point to a second wave of thought and change following the First World War. This was mostly under Roman Catholic scholarship and was marked by increased interest in patristic times of the early centuries of Christianity rather than in the medieval focus of the 19th century liturgical movement.

The second wave had the interesting effect of shifting liturgical interest away from Luther's time back further to those earliest centuries. By the 1950's and 60's the movement was so strong that if advocates showed something was done in the fourth century, they generally could get acceptance by receptive church leaders. Patrick Kiefert quotes a liturgical scholar in a session introducing the *Lutheran Book of Worship*: "One must choose one's century. It is time Lutherans stopped making the sixteenth century their norm and chose the fourth! That is what the LBW does."[16]

This second wave explains a visible yet little understood shift in vestments for Lutheran worship. In the 1950's and 60's the black cassock and white surplice largely replaced the black gown that was by far most common among Lutheran pastors up until after the Second World War. This was explainable by restoration to Luther's time. But then in the 1970's the simpler white alb with rope belt became fashionable and is now all but ubiquitous. Few were and are aware that the latest fashion represented a shift to the fourth century as the key reference point.

Such is restoration. The fourth century is now better than the sixteenth. Now, how about the first century? So far there is an aversion in Lutheran circles to push the restoration reference point all the way back to the beginnings of the Christian church. But that reference point becomes more compelling in The Other Story.

The next major step in the Restoration was the *Service Book and Hymnal* of 1958, which established the common liturgy that became the blending and unification of traditions that most of the by-then merged Lutheran churches could agree upon. Hence the importance of that year in the Restoration Story.

One more round of consolidation was supposed to include the largest group not folded into that 1958 achievement, the Lutheran Church--Missouri Synod, and was supposed to appear as the *Lutheran Book of Worship* of all Lutherans in America. Shortly before the end of this project the Missouri Synod withdrew and followed the 1978 release of *Lutheran Book of Worship* with its own nearly-the-same version, *Lutheran Worship*, in 1982.

Thus the ultimate happy ending did not happen and will not happen—at least in terms of organizational merger. But since the two service books present worship forms, settings and graphics that are virtually the same in great detail, the champions of this cause can say that the happy ending to the Worship Restoration Story has been achieved. There is something recognized as Lutheran worship that prevails across almost all expressions of Lutheranism in North America.

Of the basic content of these twin service books can be said what Luther Reed declared of the predecessor 1958 Service Book:

> (It) is a flexible and powerful instrument for the promotion of church consciousness, unity and loyalty. Intelligent and general use of it will harmonize and unify the church in a constructive development which has the promise of permanence because it is doctrinally and historically grounded, comprehensive and consistent. Individualism and provincialism must give way before an informed church consciousness of significant dimensions. Close and constant familiarity with these beautiful forms, as with fine models in art and literature will elevate standards of churchly appreciation and taste and train coming generations in practical churchmanship... (It) will be as important an instrument for these churches as the Anglican Prayer Book and the Roman Missal are in their respective communions.[17]

What a crock of Platitudes!

Now the champions of this story can relax. The job is done. Or is it?

Adaptation: The Other Story

As we have seen, the Restoration Story of worship forms dominant in Lutheran circles in America today has a beginning (Luther preserves the Mass), a middle (centuries of degeneration), and an end (restoration triumphant in current service books).

When you hear a story of heroes overcoming villains against the odds, do you wonder if there is another side to the story that deserves looking at? You should. For myself, years of research and practical administrative experience have taught me that there is usually a second or a third version that is well worth listening to before drawing conclusions. In fact, the more one-sided a story is ("We have it right and the others are all wrong."), the more important it is to look farther. Otherwise the risks of embarrassment in action on the first story are high.

The Other Beginning

The beginning of the Other Story was and remains Luther's work in the Reformation. The reference point does not shift to some other century between the first and the sixteenth—the only centuries that until recently have been considered authoritative in Lutheranism.

That Luther chose to retain a purified Mass form is a fact. The Restoration Story explained that decision by his recognition that it was "a supreme, perfected form of devotion." However, as Vilmos Vajta's research reported in the previous chapter shows, the basic rationale was Luther's strong love for the people weak in faith who were already experiencing chaos in the Reformation; they did not need any more externalities changed on them than necessary.[18] As James F. White explains, the historical ceremonies and rites "were firmly lodged in popular piety, and Luther saw no need to trample on them."[19]

Luther's reforms revolved around the impact of justification by grace through faith and thus focused on what was within the believer. By theological necessity, he had little interest in reforming personal piety through externalities, as a shuffling of rites might try to do. Again, White: "Luther's genius as a reformer was that he could approach worship reform fully aware of what a Saxon peasant brought to worship and experienced there. Because Luther wanted to reshape piety, not destroy it, he was reluctant to make changes that would scandalize the laity."[20] The respected Reformation historian E. G. Schwiebert documents how:

> The Deutsche Messe was regarded by Luther as a kind of colorful Sunday dress for those not yet strong enough in the faith. In time he hoped to dispense with the outward glitter and display of vestments, incense, candles, etc. and to provide more mature congregations with simple preaching, prayers and hymn singing; but unfortunately he did not yet have a congregation ready for removal of such props.[21]

The Restoration Story suggests that Luther had to be forced to present a simplified mass in German because he knew it would detract from the real, the full Latin mass. The Other Story is that Luther indeed felt forced and reluctant, but that was because he feared that anything he presented would be taken as an ideal pattern for every Lutheran church to follow. As with his Latin Mass titled "For the Church at Wittenberg," what he drew up this time again was meant for Wittenberg. (He wrote to a colleague, "In time I hope to have a German mass in Wittenberg that has a genuine style."[22]) Most important was to design worship with due regard for local customs and needs. Vajta demonstrates that Luther was also skeptical about working out a church constitution in detail for fear other churches would adopt it and thus disregard existing customs within the congregation and would fail to adapt to the given situation, perhaps even succumbing to legalism.[23]

Luther feared widespread uniformity, a characteristic that restorationist Lutherans have made central to their American campaigns of this century. He saw two dangers. One is legalism, which strikes at the heart of Lutheranism. The other is failure to adapt to the needs of those being serviced.

Vajta documents how "all (Luther's) liturgical reforms betray his concern for the spiritual well-being of the weak in faith. They needed a form of service which would provide for the edification without being bound to a single pattern."[24] Vajta cites a study by Allwohn offering many examples of Luther's consistent application of this principle and his conclusion that to Luther an absolute liturgical fixation was wrong in principle. Remember from the previous chapter Vajta's citation of Luther's view that neighborly love will call for many changes in forms of worship, even as a tree sprouts new blooms and fruits every years.

Writing in 1963, Franz Lau directly challenges the Restorationists' thesis that a distinctly Lutheran liturgy appeared in Luther's time that was and remains normative for all Lutheran worship. Of Luther he notes that creating a uniform liturgy was by no means his desire because, "Outward things should remain free, and the truth that the unity of the church consists in the one faith in the one gospel, not in the uniformity of outward forms in worship, should not be obscured."[25] Lau adds insight from actual practice at Luther's time:

> Against this opinion (that there was a distinctly Lutheran liturgy that should remain normative) stands the fact that large and important parts of the church in Germany which

became Lutheran—Wuerttemberg, the Upper German cities, and in particular Strassburg—introduced a completely different type of liturgy. Here the Sunday worship was not at all based upon the Mass, but upon a special late-medieval liturgical form, the preaching service, consisting only of a sermon in a simple framework of prayers and hymns; meanwhile, the Lord's Supper was connected with still another model entirely different from the Roman Mass; an independent late-medieval Communion service. Differences between Luther and the aforementioned churches never arose from the fact that the congregational worship on Sundays was conducted in Wuerttemberg or Strassburg in a completely different form from that used in Wittenberg. It is very dubious, therefore, to speak of 'the Lutheran liturgy" in a fixed and normative sense.[26]

Recall the Restorationists starting claim that Luther retained the historical mass because he recognized it as a supreme form of devotion perfected by centuries of thought. Such interpretation is challenged by the editor of Luther's works on liturgy and hymns, Ulrich S. Leupold. He states that

> This whole idea of restoring the sunken glory of ancient ritual is a product of nineteenth-century Romanticism and was as foreign to Luther as to the Romanist theologians of his day. He and the defenders of the Roman mass knew no other liturgical forms from which to start than the ones in actual use in the sixteenth century. ... Luther would have been somewhat nonplused by the plaudits of those who pay tribute to his conservatism, as though the preservation of ancient forms was a liturgical mark of merit.[27]

The Other Middle

The Formula of Concord of 1580 is an acknowledgment of the fact and even the desirability of diversity of worship forms. Again, the basic principle of Lutheran worship is that 'the community of God in every place and at every time has the right, authority, and power to change, reduce or to increase ceremonies according to its circumstances."

Luther Reed's restorationist work recounts how by 1555 there were already 135 different church orders which included an "agenda" or order of service. This number does not include the Lutheran churches in Scandinavia. Their service orders were similar in following roughly the order of the German Mass, but varied considerably in detail. The process continued. Lutheran historian E. Clifford Nelson estimates that by the 19th century there were 75 different hymnbooks in Saxony alone![28]

One reason for the diversity and the move away from the fuller Latin Mass is not picked up in the usual Restoration Story. By the time of the 1580 Formula of Concord, it had become important to avoid the appearance of being Roman Catholic. Thus Principle 4 in Article X says, "Likewise we hold it to be a culpable sin when in a period of persecution (which they were in) anything is done in deed or action to please enemies of the Gospel contrary and in opposition to the Christian confession, whether in things indifferent, in doctrine, or in whatever else pertains to religion."[29]

For centuries to come this principle of not pleasing "enemies of the Gospel" meant avoiding the appearance of being Roman Catholic, and avoiding such appearance was a dominant theme in Lutheranism. I personally can remember it as a concern in my childhood in Cleveland Lutheranism. Somehow in recent decades this principle has been left behind. Ecumenism had something to do with it. But liturgical development was probably more significant. It is certainly worth debate whether upholding or forgetting the principle is more authentically Lutheran.

For present purposes we pick up the story of adaptation with the movement of Lutherans across the ocean to North America in various waves of immigration. In the Restoration Story, worship practices really deteriorated under primitive and pioneer conditions. That is a view of established, later generations. As sort of a starting point for the long journey upwards, Restorationists can point to Henry Muhlenberg's journal entry of 1748, where he describes how difficult it was to develop a common liturgy for the Ministerium of Pennsylvania because "almost every town and village had its own."[30]

The Other Story sees this as a time of tremendous mission outreach to newcomers in new places with often little more in common than a language which was not the dominant one in the new country. For many immigrants church life in the old country had not been a significant part of their life except in often-forced social externalities. In the freedom of the new land they did not automatically gravitate to the local church of their tradition or set one up if it had not yet appeared. Missionaries and new congregations had to work hard to reach out and to attract these nominal Lutherans to church life that could no longer be imposed.

Of necessity in those circumstances, pastors and church leaders concentrated on the spiritual basics of personal salvation and spiritual security. Of necessity, worship was simple and to the point. Ritual was a secondary concern. Church historians estimate that only one out of four immigrants from heavily Lutheran areas in the old country wound up associating themselves with a Lutheran congregation in the new country.

Often the people most active in founding and developing Lutheran congregations could be described as pietists. They took personal spiritual piety very seriously, which of course also became a basic motivation for mission. The major leader of the 18th century, Henry Muhlenberg, was sent out from the pietist center in Halle, Germany, and Pietism has been traced as a major influence among colonial Lutherans.[31] The core group that formed the Lutheran Church--Missouri Synod was originally led by a prominent pietist leader from Dresden. While his followers, especially C.F.W. Walther, reacted against the excesses of uncertainty in what they had experienced, the first generation leaders of the Missouri Synod all carried strong pietist influences and orientation with them. Large proportions of Norwegians, Swedes and Danes had been touched by pietist movements in their home country and carried this perspective with them in their religion and church values. In comparison to the Germans, the Scandinavians tended to manifest a more pietistic spirit.[32] Again, those with pietistic orientation could be expected to put more effort into founding and developing churches.

The reason to highlight the formative influence of Pietism in North American Lutheranism is that the Restoration Story counts this movement as one of the culprits in the decline of liturgy. Indeed, Lutheran historian Abdel Wenz points out that in the early periods of Lutheranism in America, under pietist influences, "There was a constant tendency...in the direction of less formality, less conformity to the church year, more extempore prayers with intercessions for definite individuals, and more adaptation to circumstances."[33] Many would ask today whether these tendencies were a weakness or a strength.

[handwritten margin note: Right On! Don't we wish all churches did this!]

There is an inherent tension between a focus on worship ritual and a focus on personal response. Pietists tend to worry that an emphasis on ritual will lead to reliance on external church formalities that can let personal spiritual life and response to Word and sacraments go stale or slack. Those who emphasize assuringly familiar formalities and ritual for presenting Word and sacraments worry that a stress on response at the feeling level may do a disservice to those who are led to think they should gauge their spiritual life according to their enthusiasm or other emotions, leaving them exposed to times of uncertainty or even despair when they experience low levels of emotion that make them doubt their relationship with God.

[handwritten margin note: Here is some of the problem.]

In the tension between the objective and subjective in worship, each side has the strength of what it emphasizes but then also the potential weakness of what is left assumed and unemphasized. The constant challenge is to develop worship practices that incorporate and balance both sets of strengths. The earlier liturgical renewal movement and now the contemporary worship movement each aim at overcoming the contrasting set of weaknesses that worship leaders want to address.

If you, the reader, are attracted to the Other Story and its significant phase of Pieteism, you should know that Pietism has become somewhat of a dirty word in Lutheran leadership circles in the past several generations of ascendancy of the Restoration Story. Few have been willing to say good words about what truly was a necessary, strong and positive force in American Lutheranism.

The tension between the formality of liturgical ritual and the emotionalism of Pietism remains at the heart of current concerns about the future for Lutheranism in America. Pietism essentially continues its existence in much of current American Evangelicalism.

Elsewhere I have made the case for how churches can retain Lutheran substance while developing aspects of Evangelical style.[34]

The point at hand is simply to counter the Restoration Story's negative view of Pietism with the Other Story's positive view of its impact on effective mission outreach.

As Lutherans scattered themselves across North America in the 18th and 19th centuries, they formed many associations, or synods of like-minded congregations of similar language. Some of those early associations had pietistic characteristics as a unifying concern. It would be instructive to track their growth rate in comparison to the other groups. But in the 20th century the overarching drive towards unity brought a complex array of mergers, so that distinctive features have gotten lost.

A Case Study

There is only one major grouping of Lutherans in America that was never involved in significant mergers. It provides an interesting test case. This is the Lutheran Church--Missouri Synod. Today it composes roughly one third of Lutheranism in America.

In his 1955 history of Lutheranism in America, Abdel Wentz describes the Missouri Synod as "one of the most vigorous elements in American Christianity."[35] He attributes this to their rapid growth in numbers and expansion in territory, their contagious enthusiasm for conservative evangelical doctrine, their constant emphasis on thorough educational methods, and their relatively large supply of ministerial candidates.

One other element Wentz could have added. In his 1923 history, *The Lutheran Church in American History*, Wentz picked two characteristics to feature in describing this church body in the 19th century. They were "characterized by their intense pietism and their strict Lutheran orthodoxy."[36] It is interesting that by 1955 Wentz dropped the pietists part of the story. In his 1955 account, though, he does acknowledge how these Germans loved "the fervor of their religious hymns and the deep inwardness of their devotional literature."[37]

That orthodoxy is central to its identity is well recognized in the history of the Missouri Synod. The pietist characteristics have become like a relative the family is ashamed of and doesn't talk about any more. Most of the official writings concentrated on asserting and defending Lutheran orthodoxy, which was a constant in leadership forums. But at the level of routine congregational life, the emphasis tended to be personalistic, stressing personal piety and social morality and the continual proclamation of the presence of a loving God.[38]

American Lutheran church historian James Albers cites four characteristics of 19th-century Missouri Synod churches that reflected pietistic leanings. Many of the Synod's clergy came from pietist centers or were especially affected by the pietist Awakening Movement of the 1820's-30's in Germany. While ever vigilant to avoid validating religious authority on feeling or emotions, the formative leader of that century, C.F.W.Walther, through his own personal experience, maintained a life-long appreciation of the fact that often the grace of God comes crashing into one's life through a powerful experience resembling a rebirth.

Albers also notes how confirmation was a powerful spiritual experience for several generations of the church body's young people. A third characteristic is the proliferation of ministry and service societies and associations like those developed in earlier pietist times in Germany. Finally, like Pietism, the Missouri Synod placed a strong emphasis on the role of laity in the church.[39]

The two thrusts were well blended. The orthodoxy with its central emphasis on justification by grace cautioned against the potential excesses of Pietism. And there is much to be cautious about. But the popular piety kept the orthodoxy from becoming lifeless and was significant in energizing what became "one of the most vigorous elements in American Christianity."

The Missouri Synod has been relatively late to and has exercised little leadership in the movement to more refined liturgy among American Lutherans. This is partially because the church body was late in changing to English, and then just adopted basically the English language Common Service of 1888. But it is also because, until lately, liturgy just was not very important in the relative scale of what motivated leadership. Orthodoxy and mission expansion were higher concerns against a background of general pietistic indifference to liturgy.

This relative lack of interest is reflected in recorded correspondence between Luther Reed and Synodical President John W. Behnken in 1946. Crusader Reed wrote to invite the Missouri Synod to participate in fashioning a common liturgy. Behnken wrote back that the Synodical Conference had just published a new hymnal (the 1942 *Lutheran Hymnal* still used in about 40% of the congregations) which contains a liturgy that was getting extensive use and "which is being introduced in many places where very little liturgy formerly was in use." Having, let alone refining a special liturgy just was not very important.[40]

By today's standards the 1942 hymnal presents a simple liturgy. At that, many pastors did not use all of it. But it was a significant change from the even simpler order of service of the German hymnal officially published by the Synod as late as 1917. The simple order in the 1917 German service book (two very small pages without communion, three and a half with) was a pattern of song, greeting, Scripture reading, song, sermon, prayers, song and benediction, interspersed with a few antiphons, which are a one sentence statement and response. It is essentially the basic service (three songs and a sermon, plus some prayers) that can be seen in most established Protestant churches in this country. Noteworthy is that the confession of sins comes immediately after the sermon (rather than at the beginning of the service) as a form of response. Response to the sermon is something other Protestants tend to look for but has become a lost expectation in English-language Lutheran services, except perhaps in the weakened form of an offering and, in the latest settings, in the creed. Also interesting in the German service is that while there is provision for announcements, the gathering of an offering is not mentioned.[41]

How much was added when going to the English language is apparent in the *Evangelical Lutheran Hymn-Book*, published in English by Concordia Publishing House about the same time, in 1918. The equally small print on small pages now totaled eleven pages without communion and eighteen with.[42] It is essentially the same rite and rubrics as in *The Lutheran Hymnal* of 1942.

Frequency of the Lord's Supper

As most Lutheran orders did until recently, these 1917 and 1918 orders separated out as an addendum on a special page what the remaining service would be when communion is celebrated. While the communion rite is usually at the center of discussion in liturgical circles, it did not receive as much attention in earlier times because communion was infrequently observed and was thus a special circumstance. That it be properly observed with correct theology and preparation was very important. But the ritual around the simple Words of Institution was of secondary concern.

Today the frequency of celebration of the Lord's Supper is one of the key issues in defining Lutheran worship. The liturgical movement has propagated a value assumption that has gone largely unchallenged, although not always followed. To be truly Lutheran, the premise goes, a congregation has to celebrate the eucharist weekly. Anything less means there is more ground to cover in overcoming the forces of degeneration.

This premise is based on the starting point that Luther used the Latin Mass and later the German Mass, which by definition included the Lord's Supper. Remember, opinions differ about whether he offered this as a model. In any event, how extensively did Lutherans in that golden time participate in communion? More important, how long did this practice last? There is good reason to observe that widespread participation was not common and that the full service, with communion, did not last many decades in actual congregational usage. Thus, is weekly communion really normative for Lutheran worship?

Franz Lau urges caution about "historical fables" that the sacramental service was the only proper Lutheran service:

> Even on historical grounds this is not correct. The worship life as it took shape under Luther's influence was very rich. Every Sunday several worship services took place.... These were preaching services! ... That the services under the influence of Luther and Wittenberg were in a majority of instances sacramental services is a historical fable and nothing more.[43]

Before the Reformation, the mass was indeed celebrated frequently, even daily in church. But it had become something done by priests, often alone. It's sacrificial nature did not necessitate involvement of the ordinary people, who usually were just observers of the ritual performed around the altar and might individually receive the sacrament only a few times a year.[44] Reformation theology eliminated the sacrificial nature of this sacrament and focused on it as a means of grace to be received individually. But this basic shift in theology did not mean that popular perception of the use of this part of the service changed quickly or extensively. Indeed James White offers this observation of the century following Luther's death:

> Gradually, tying celebrations to the presence of communicants led to less frequent eucharists. The shift to frequent reception of the communion had been too radical a change from medieval practices for the laity to become accustomed to it easily. As a result, the first half of the service, the ante-communion, came to be the usual Sunday celebration, the full eucharist becoming the exceptional service....[45]

Another reason for this shift toward doing just the first part of the service was the rise in importance of preaching. Before the Reformation the mass provided for only short comments on the assigned readings. In contrast, as Werner Elert in his interpretation of Luther's theology declares, "the preaching and teaching of God's Word is the main part of all divine service."[46] Is it still today?

Yet another reason for decreased frequency is that individual confession and absolution was tied into worthy reception of the sacrament. This led to a time-consuming process that meant days and even weeks of pastoral time devoted to necessary preparation of individuals for their personal worthy celebration of the Lord's Supper. It is understandable how quarterly celebration became the norm.

But probably a major reason the usual service was without communion is a popular desire for simplicity. The Reformed leader John Calvin, we are told, personally to the end of his life desired a weekly communion. But he was overruled by the civil magistracy in Geneva, which imposed a quarterly practice.[47] Quarterly communion is often referred to as a Reformed practice. They, too, did practice it. But the motivation does not appear to be theological. In effect, it was something the lay leadership wanted for simplicity, and probably also to shorten the service. This same mentality undoubtedly prevailed in cities where Lutheranism was dominant, with similar result.

In recent decades Restoration advocates have prevailed with the ideology of weekly communion for truly Lutheran worship. As we have seen, their claim that this was the norm at Luther's time is certainly questionable. But even if their claim for those first several decades of the Reformation stood, what about the 400 years between those first decades and the recent ones? The complete dominance of less than weekly communion during this history does leave questionable the premise that the only true Lutheran worship is the mass focused on celebration of the Lord's Supper.

But maybe for most of those years Lutheran leaders really did not understand Lutheran theology. They were duped by Reformed tendencies, or by Pietism, or by Rationalism, so the claim goes. But what about those whose Lutheran orthodoxy is beyond reproach and who knew what they were doing in comparison to Reformed churches? What about C.F.W. Walther, the dominant Lutheran theologian and churchman in America in the 19th century? In his pastorate he practiced quarterly communion, like almost all of the other Lutheran churches of his time.

If frequency of celebration of communion is the measure of how Lutheran a church's worship is, then my contemporary service with monthly communion is clearly more Lutheran than the worship of the mother church of the Missouri Synod!

In view of the realities of Lutheran history, how can anyone insist that the "mass" is the only true form of Lutheran worship?

The Other Ending

The Other Story does not have an ending. Because of its nature, one should not expect an ending either. As cultures and times change, so worship goes through adaptation to meet the needs of the people being served.

But the Other Story is undergoing a bit of a resurgence. This is the meaning of the movement toward contemporary worship. American culture of the 1990's is very different from the culture of the 1950's, when television communication was still young, and even more different from the culture of the turn of the century, when ethnic identity and languages other than English were still dominant in the heartland of Lutheranism. It is not unreasonable to anticipate that what is effective in worship practices will also change—especially in churches that take seriously a sense of mission to people who are shaped by the current culture and have no previous exposure to Lutheran traditions.

Notes

[1] Luther D. Reed, *The Lutheran Liturgy,* rev., ed., Muhlenberg Press, 1959, p. 188.
[2] Ibid., p. 70.
[3] Ibid., p. 76.
[4] Ibid., p. 79.
[5] Ibid., p. 109.
[6] Ibid., p. 143.
[7] Ibid., p. 146.
[8] Ibid., p. 148.
[9] Ibid., p. 82.
[10] Ibid., p. 196.
[11] Ibid., p. 150.
[12] Ibid., p. 189.
[13] Ibid., p. 189.
[14] Ibid., p. 180.
[15] Gracia Grindal, "Faithful in the Face of Change," *Word and World,*, Vol XII, No. 3, (Summer 1992), p. 225.
[16] Patrick R. Kiefert, *Welcoming the Stranger,* Augsburg, 1992, p. 42.
[17] Reed, op. cit., pp. 222, 223.
[18] Vilmos Vajta, *Luther on Worship,* Muhlenberg Press, 1959, p. 174.
[19] James F. White, *Protestant Worship: Traditions in Transition,* Westminster/John Knox Press, 1989, p. 43.
[20] Ibid., p. 43.
[21] E. G. Schwiebert, *Luther And His Times: The Reformation From a New Perspective,* Concordia, 1950 p. 668.
[22] cited in Ulrich S. Leupold's Introduction to ."The German Mass and Order of Service," in *Luther's Works, Volume 53: Liturgy and Hymns,* ed by Ulrich S. Leupold, Fortress, Press, 1965, p. 54.
[23] Vajta, op. cit., p. 182.

[24] Ibid., p. 180.

[25] Franz Lau, *Luther*, trans by Robert H. Fischer, Westminster, 1953, p. 98.

[26] Ibid., p. 99.

[27] Leupold's edition of *Luther's Work*, op. cit., p. xiv.

[28] E. Clifford Nelson, ed., *The Lutherans in North America*, Rev. ed., Fortress Press, 1980, p. 206.

[29] "Apology of the Augsburg Confession," *The Book of Concord*, trans and ed by Theodore G. Tappert, Muhlenberg Press, 1959.

[30] Reed, op. cit., p. 164.

[31] Theodore G. Tappert, "The Influence of Pietism in Colonial Lutheranism," in *Continental Pietism and Early American Christianity*, ed F. Ernest Stoeffler, Eerdmans, 1976, pp. 13-33.

[32] Eugene L Fevold, "Coming of Age, 1875-1900, in *The Lutherans in North America*, ed. by E Clifford Nelson, rev. ed, Fortress, 1980, p. 351.

[33] Abdel Ross Wentz, *A Basic History of Lutheranism in America*, rev. ed., Fortress Press, 1964, p. 58.

[34] David S. Luecke, *Evangelical Style and Lutheran Substance*, Concordia, 1988.

[35] Wentz, *A Basic History*, op. cit., p. 220.

[36] Abdel Ross Wentz, *The Lutheran Church in American History*, United Lutheran Publishing House, 1923, p. 151.

[37] Wentz, *A Basic History*, op. cit., p. 214.

[38] Interview in June 1986 and follow-up letter of Feb. 23, 1988, from James W. Albers, associate professor of theology, Valparaiso University.

[39] James W. Albers, "Lutheranism and Pietism, *The Lutheran Historical Conference Essays and Reports of the Meeting of November, 1990*, Vol XIV (1992) p. 165-168.

[40] Reed, op. cit., p. 208.

[41] *Kirchengesangbuch fuer Evangelisch-Lutherische Gemeinden*, Concordia Publishing House, 1917, pp III-VI.

[42] *Evangelical Lutheran Hymn-Book*, Concordia Publishing House, 1918, pp. 1-18.

[43] Franz Lau, op cit., p. 100.

[44] James F. White, *Protestant Worship: Traditions in Transition*, Westminster/John Knox, 1989, p. 42.

[45] White, op. cit., p. 50.

[46] Werner Elert, *The Structure of Lutheranism*, Vol 1, trans. by Walter A Hansen, Concordia Publishing House, 1962, p. 324.

[47] Reed, op. cit., p. 83.

Chapter 7

Is There Room for Popular Culture in Lutheran Worship?

> You must have noticed how churches and movements of a pronounced evangelical note manifest the most shocking musical taste.... Look at the abominations of the Billy Graham Song Book.... It is a miserable confession to have to make, but it is none the less the fact that many of our liveliest churches show themselves to be full of the most outrageous error as soon as they open their mouths in song.

Thus says church musician and professor Erik Routley in his 1960 collection of essays *Music Sacred and Profane.*[1]

Thus we begin a discussion of an aspect of a church's worship life that is seldom clearly labeled for what it is. This is culture—defined here as matters of taste and preference in aesthetic expressions, specifically in music, literature, and art. Different preferences can be called different styles of expression. This puts us squarely in the middle of issues of styles of worship.

Eric Routley represents what we can call <u>high culture</u>--carefully refined tastes according to high standards established by a specialized elite as the best. Classical music of former centuries is an easily recognized form of high culture. One approach to the music dimension of worship is to depend on a musician and/or music director specially trained to know "the best" church musical literature and to perform it in exceptional ways.

Contemporary music in the current worship movement represents <u>popular culture,</u> which is usually different from high culture. Music you hear on most-listened-to radio stations is popular culture. Looking at "the charts" to see which praise songs are most frequently used in churches reflects a popular culture perspective in churches.

You determine which music people like most in worship and do more of it.

There is usually a tension between preferences for high culture and for popular culture. This tension is often at the heart of conflict over worship in Lutheran churches today. There may be attempts to cover it with theological dressing, but in most cases the tension is basically over issues of aesthetics.

Eric Routley gives the high culture version of the issue when he observes "that in ordinary congregations there remains a tension between what the musicians are sure represents the best in music and what they are assured by others that 'the people want'." Thus he worries about tolerating church music that remains second rate.

Routley is fun to begin with because he pushes the elitist's perspective to a "shocking" extreme when he talks about "the most shocking musical taste," "the abominations of the Billy Graham Song Book," and lively churches that show "the most outrageous error as soon as they open their mouths to sing."

Here is a response from a popular culture perspective. Such condescension raises questions about his basic understanding of congregational worship—and about the attitude of musical worship leaders who tolerate and even encourage such an air of superiority. It borders on Phariseeism. Snobbery is another word for it. It's hard to imagine Jesus or the apostles having much patience with this dismissal of sincere worship of ordinary people.

Characteristic of the culture issue is that elitist Eric Routley's caustic barbs are dropped on churches that emphasize evangelism and liveliness. These churches have a clear purpose of reaching out to others, and they shape their preferences in taste accordingly. They tend to favor music and formats that are easily understood and appreciated by ordinary people without the need for specially developed taste. In other words, they lean toward popular culture. This is offensive to high-culture elitists.

To update terminology, church leaders intentionally pursuing church growth strategies look for user-friendly forms and music that can support the worship experience of people with little church experience. Popular contemporary Christian music thus becomes attractive. Traditionalists often don't like this approach—for reasons that usually stay at the level of feeling that "church shouldn't be done that way."

The rationale for leaning toward popular culture expressions of music in church seems clear to me. This is a natural development for a church with a high priority on outreach and evangelism. The rationale for high culture in churches has something to do with offering "the best." But defining "the best" leads into some complicated issues that often are left unexamined until questions of purpose for a church's worship are raised.

I will try to identify rationales for traditional emphasis on high culture in churches and then discuss some of the inconsistencies this yields.

Does Bach Make For Better Worship?

One avowed critic of church growth approaches is former Lutheran Richard John Neuhaus. In making a general criticism of "the church growth movement" he approaches matters of taste in worship head on.

Neuhaus worries that some worship services can be "well, tacky." Appreciation for excellence in taste is not snobbery, he claims; it is discernment. The beautiful as well as the good and the true are matters of judgment, and mature human beings should have the confidence to recommend their judgments to others. Furthermore, in his view, to fudge elementary judgments in these areas is to render a grievous disservice to the Christian people. Neuhaus offers this tantalizing position: "Yes, the eucharistic liturgy is superior to programmed spiritual excitements, Bach is superior to rock, and Luther's theology to Robert Schuller's."[2]

In matters of truth, undoubtedly Luther's theology is superior. This can be demonstrated Scripturally.

But how does one demonstrate that Bach is superior to rock? More to the point, what is the proof the eucharistic liturgy is superior to all forms of "programmed spiritual excitements"?

Should we imagine God in heaven looking down on a Sunday worship service at a church in Brecksville, or Brownsville, or Oceanside and concluding, "That was more pleasing to me than last week; the organist did two Bach pieces and they sang Luther and Gerhardt hymns—but I still wish they would get a real organ."

Or should we picture God as disappointed one Sunday because the Lord's Supper wasn't celebrated with an Agnus Dei and a full eucharistic prayer?

Or does God feel less worshiped when after the sermon participants are involved in 10 minutes of halting, simple small group prayers rather than hearing the pastor read an eloquent prayer?

To me, the answer is apparent. The God of the New Testament is not nearly as impressed with the externalities of the forms worshipers use as with how internalized and heartfelt their engagement with him is in their acts of worship. I think he is more disappointed with worship that becomes mostly rote or without personal engagement, regardless of how refined, than with worship that may lack musical or literary sophistication but freshly touches the worshipers.

Jesus emphasized that God is much more impressed with the simple prayer of a simple repentant sinner than with the liturgically correct prayer of the Pharisee. He wants souls that acknowledge him as the center of their being, that are moved to stand in awe of him. God wants to be worshiped in spirit and in truth. The Apology to the Augsburg Confession interprets this to mean God should be worshiped with the heart. He looks less for the compositional and performance merits of what is said or sung than for the heart condition represented by the saying or singing.

How does Bach fit into these consideration? It seems to me the theologically proper question for evaluating his contribution is whether his music and chorale settings touch hearts and move spirits. For some people this undoubtedly happens, and then their worship can have extra layers of God-pleasing meaning and richness. But this is most likely to happen for those who have grown up listening to Bach on organs in churches and who thus find the sounds bringing associations from past experiences, and especially for those who know well the hymns set in his chorale preludes. Yes, Bach can be great—for those with the church and musical conditioning to appreciate his sophistication.

Long may high-culture worship continue to be offered in Lutheran churches. But only this and none other? Can't there also be popular culture alternatives offered by churches that are doctrinally Lutheran?

What about ministry to those who have not grown up in a church listening to specialized music and who thus do not bring past associations to such a listening experience? For many, a simpler music with repetitive lyrics and a clear beat can be better heart music supportive of worshipful engagement with God. In many situations, reliance on Bach or other high culture contributors can yield superficial worship not particularly pleasing to God or of value to the worshiper. Must our message be, Hang in there until you learn to like it?

These observations come from someone who has relatively mature musical judgment. I have grown up in Lutheran churches, schools and colleges, singing in concert choirs and playing church trumpet repertoire. I studied classical organ. I am musically most comfortable in high culture. My car radio stays tuned to either of the two local classical music stations, and I keep a season subscription to the opera. But I know enough about high culture to realize that I cannot realistically aspire to impose it on everyone, especially in matters as serious as ministry and as personal as worship.

Is Bach better than rock? You have to answer that by first deciding, for whom and for what purpose. For someone whose musical experience is limited to what can be heard on popular radio (which describes two thirds of the American population), Bach is not likely to be associated with a moving heartfelt religious experience. Well done Christian music that picks up some of the melodic contours, rhythms, and harmonies of popular music would have a better chance. And I do know people for whom Christian rock is a very moving worship experience.

For me personally, Bach remains better than most rock. But that is beside the point. As a pastor, I do not pick Sunday worship music for my own tastes. And those are not the only options. I am convinced that for the unchurched people I am trying to reach today in this community, some Jack Hayford, Michael W. Smith, or Twilla Paris (hardly rock) is better music for church than most J. S. Bach. The more I work with contemporary music, the more I am struck by the way many Scripture-based Christian choruses can regularly touch hearts, also of long-churched Lutherans, and can engage par-

102

ticipants from many backgrounds in a worshipful relationship of thanksgiving and praise to God for all the Scripturally right reasons.

Focusing on the Right Gap
between Church and Community

Richard John Neuhaus offered the judgment of comparisons just discussed. What was for him elementary turns out to be simplistic. He offers another observation that is worth a few more paragraphs.

Neuhaus goes on to proclaim that there should be and must be a communication gap between the church and the broader community. This is in response to a church growth caution about opening up a communication gap by pursuing personal maturity (as in musical sensibilities) at the expense of ongoing evangelism.

Here is Neuhaus' reasoning: "If there is no communication gap, it is only because the church has nothing to communicate that is significantly different from the culture. Christianity is a distinctive worldview, with a distinctive vocabulary, distinctive moral sensibilities, and a distinctive way of being in the world. It is ... a cultural-linguistic tradition. One must be initiated into it, one must make a decision about it, one must cross the gap into another world."[3]

Communicating the Gospel is indeed difficult, but we need to realize that the gap remains basically spiritual. When the Holy Spirit bridges that gap of faith, a Christian's new life in Christ should yield distinctive moral sensibilities and ways of being in the world. But is a distinctive vocabulary and "cultural-linguistic tradition" essential to the gap? Or does that distinctive tradition itself often become an impediment and create a false communication gap?

God's Word in Scripture remains fundamental to the communication. But for 99% of the world's population, the Greek words of the original have to be translated, and in recent centuries preferably into something other than Latin. Are we somehow to believe that the Holy Spirit can work best through words that retain traditional Greek and Latin derivations? It seems much wiser to choose words, forms, and expressions that can be more readily understood by the people we are talking to, whether or not they already have a specialized church background.

After all, what is the "it" into which one must be initiated and cross the gap? Neuhaus and many who like the high-culture approach come dangerously close to seeing "it" as the church with its cultural-linguistic tradition, including music and art. But such would be more a Roman Catholic view with an emphasis on salvation in the church. Faithful followers of Luther have to see "it" as Jesus Christ and to focus on most effectively preparing the way for the Holy Spirit to initiate or build up a person into new spiritual life in Christ. That is the other world to cross into or to be elevated into, not the world of externalities accumulated by churches over the centuries. If a decision has to be made, this should be about following Christ in faith and action, not about fitting into a church with all its specialized musical and linguistic cultural tradition.

In fact, one can make the case that the distinctiveness of church tradition often works against the kind of discipleship God is looking for. The "it" of following Christ should be something that happens seven days a week in all aspects of daily living. The more discipleship is linked with an unusual church culture of specialized vocabulary, music, art, and decorum, the easier it is for Christian life to become something compartmentalized and done only Sundays "in church." Then a church culture has evolved into something counterproductive to the authentic Christian living in the kingdom of God. This is more likely to happen in pursuit of high culture that models a kingdom separate from the rule of God in the lives of ordinary people with ordinary tastes and vocabulary.

Here is a simple test of church culture inclinations. When you and other leaders of your church are describing the building, do you like to talk about the "narthex"? Today this usually describes the lobby or entranceway. Lutheran ministers have a strong tendency to say narthex, even though the word is not in the vocabulary of the vast majority of people in this country, not even among Christians from other heritages. How is the cause of Christ promoted by a specialized church vocabulary even in something so neutral as a building lobby? How much of an unnecessary communication gap is regularly left by promoting a church culture of insiders' arcane words the meaning of which could just as easily be expressed in vocabulary people could understand--even and especially outsiders?

Your attitude toward "narthex" probably predicts your attitude toward church culture in general--and contemporary worship in particular.

Trying To Be In But Not Of The World

One thing almost all Lutherans can agree on today is that the subject of contemporary or alternative worship raises tensions in churches and among pastors. Sometimes the tension remains at a level mostly of taste and the politics of preference. But most participants feel there is more to the issue, even if they cannot express it well.

The point of this chapter is to claim that a fundamental part of the conflict is cultural conflict. I am oversimplifying it by drawing a contrast between high culture and popular culture in the service of the Gospel.

To call the tension cultural is not to dismiss it lightly. The Scriptural expression of the issue is the challenge to be in the world but not of the world. Jesus sends his followers into the world and pointedly refrains from praying that they be taken out of the world, yet they are not to be of the world (John 17: 11-16). Specifically in relation to the spiritual act of worship, the Apostle Paul tells us to no longer conform to the pattern of this world but to be transformed by the renewing of our minds (Romans 12:2).

High culture is a way of being different from and thus not of the world, and can be seen as a contribution to transforming the mind. Popular culture purposefully goes into the world of the commonplace and familiar. Advocates of a distinctive church high culture accuse the other side of breaking the tension by becoming too much of the world. Advocates of popular culture in the church, expressed today in contemporary worship, view the traditional church culture as no longer going sufficiently into the world. Put a drum set in the "chancel," another church-culture term, and you can watch the feeling level go up on both sides, and with it the tension over worship.

Such tension over worship practices is productive. It comes with faithfulness to Jesus' expectation that we be both in but not of the world. Openness to popular culture has to be at least considered by any church wanting to be serious about effectively reaching out to the unchurched with the Gospel. But those who want to evangelize by simplifying have to worry whether their witness is becoming too diluted and they are sacrificing too much of what has proven useful over the long haul of Christian living.

On this issue I am biased toward popular culture. But I would not want to advocate this as the only way for Lutherans to worship. That would be a faulty reduction of the tension at the expense of valuable tradition that is meaningful to so many. The case for high culture and what can be lost without its strengths needs to be heard and respected, and it can be made with less condescension than conveyed by Routley or Neuhaus. But I see that the greater danger for Lutherans is a faulty reduction of the tension by insisting only on worship that is intended to stay separate from the world through a distinctive liturgical culture with its accumulations of symbols and traditions. Weaknesses to which this approach is prone need to be recognized and put in perspective when considering ministry challenges in an unchurched culture.

An Unpersuasive Case
Against Popular Church Culture

I can offer an example of faulty reasoning to be avoided when setting out a direction for being "no longer of the world" in worship. Along the way it tries to make a case against popular culture in churches. This is a recent book on *Discipling Music Ministry* by Christian college music professor Calvin M. Johansson. While he addresses specifically music, the reasoning he represents is sometimes applied as well to preference for the whole range of high-culture literary and symbolic expressions used in worship. For my understanding of discipling ministry, the case is not persuasive.

In Johansson's view a disciplining music ministry is one that brings discipline into a believer's pursuit of maturity in becoming like our Lord. He believes only music that is mature can contribute to such maturity, for music that builds on immature theoretical concepts fosters a similar condition in the listener.

In general, according to Johansson, music is disciplined and therefore is discipling ministry to the extent that it moves toward the ascetic and the austerity of self denial. Harmony which is lean and spare (like fourths and fifths) is more disciplined than lavish and rich harmonies of seconds, sixths, ninths, and thirteenths. Rhythms that lend themselves to hand clapping lack the discipline necessary for maturation. The original "rugged" rhythm of "A Mighty Fortress" is more difficult to sing but the effort is worthwhile. Polyphony (where soprano, alto, tenor, and base parts are independent melodically) is one of the most disciplined forms of music. That it is not transparent or immediately understandable is good. Johansson notes, "The compositional remoteness and disciplined distance of polyphony give to the music a certain ambiguity which reminds us of God's distance, his dissimilarity to us.... Polyphony's disposition is decidedly otherworldly."[4] Also otherworldly and therefore to be commended is Gregorian chant--a "veritable gold mine of disciplined church music."[5]

As one might guess, Johansson is not in favor of popular music in church. "Usually our sights have been set on making music comfortable and pleasing--that is, popular. In a culture with a general disregard for the highest musical quality, achieving popularity has meant sacrificing integrity."[6] Somehow in Johansson's approach, musical integrity to the highest compositional standards becomes a reflection of the spiritual integrity, or lack thereof, in a believer's Christian life.

Thus, in this view, Bach really does make for better worship. This would be Johansson's conclusion because he is convinced, "All art is based on God-given principles that are laid down in creation and are cross-cultural and timeless. As the consummate artist, God and his standards are the objective criteria by which all art is judged."[7]

A fundamental theme in Johansson's vision for music ministry is that if most people like it, it can't be good. The reason is that the call to follow Christ means self-denial. Music that people like is really giving in to the hedonistic pleasure syndrome that is the basis of humanism. It panders to self indulgence that is contradictory to the very nature of the Christian faith. Enjoyment is a false criterion for ministerial worth. "When personal gratification is worship's objective, worship is invalidated. To leave the service with the query,

'Now what did I get out of worship today,' is to misunderstand the nature of worship."[8] What makes Gregorian chant so appropriate for church music is its truly spiritual nature; it is "not made for beauty, aesthetic contemplation, enjoyment, pleasure, or emotional satisfaction."[9]

An interesting twist to Johannson's view of rugged aesthetic self denial is his call for a prophetic role for music ministry. In refusing the task of simply providing musical satisfaction, the musician should recognize that this prophetic role may necessitate going against the grain of popular trends. Sensitized to higher standards, a musician's conscience may dictate a course of action that people find unappetizing. Then "congregations must realize that such decisions are made not to spite them, but out of concern for them."[10] Progress cannot be made until the people are teachable, which can happen when they recognize in this ministry God's hand at work making the assembly after the image of his own Son.

What is your reaction so far? Mine is, "What a shallow understanding of "prophetic" to equate it with imposing anything unpopular in the name of a vague hand of God! This mindset reminds me of a popular paperback from the 1930's I found on my father's bookshelf. By Henry C. Link, it was a psychologist's call for *A Return To Religion*. That sounded promising. It turns out his case was for gaining psychological maturity and happiness by overcoming selfishness and forcing yourself to do things you don't like to do. He didn't like to go to church and assumed most others didn't, because it was so boring. But return anyhow, he said. You'll force yourself into greater maturity. Such was his role in life for religion. It is similar to Johansson's role in church for music.

What about evangelism? According to Johansson, it better produce the right kind of church members. They need to be teachable, and teaching on music ministry should be a normal topic of study for those who are taking up membership. "Unless this is done, it is difficult to achieve congregational progress, because newcomers are not properly acclimated to the goals and methodology of music ministry. They will tend therefore to slow down the progress of the congregation as a whole."[11]

Like cultural spokesman Erik Routley in the introduction, musician Calvin Johansson is a worthwhile contributor to understanding issues of worship culture because he puts into words such an extreme—and faulty—approach. Surely most church leaders would agree there is something wrong with an understanding of worship that sees newcomers as a drag on the "progress" of the congregation. Or is it just the church-growth-oriented evangelistic types who see that newcomers in themselves have something to do with reflecting the progress of a congregation. Are there really practicing leaders who want to defend the position that completion of a music-appreciation class be a pre-requisite for membership in a church? Is the case any different when the expectation is a liturgy-appreciation class?

Somehow it does not come as a surprise that Johansson's ideal for Christian maturity is medieval monasticism, where, he concludes, simplicity and submissive humility were basic to discipleship, and real discipline held life together. See the parallel that recent liturgical renewal has meant a restoration of medieval priestly worship, although of late tweaked to the fourth century.

What happened to the Reformation tide change of religious values toward affirming authentic, mature Christian living as something ordinary Christians in ordinary walks of life could achieve? Do those who pursue a high-culture approach still believe that Christian maturity is a matter of deepened spiritual response to increased Biblical understandings achieved by the Holy Spirit, or do they see maturity as primarily something achieved by only a few Christians through careful instruction in the cultural symbolisms of music, art, and literary refinement? Is Reformation theology so life-denying that there is no room for popular culture expressions of music and speech? If people clap their hands while singing in church, are they automatically selfish, pleasure-seeking immature Christians?

Is Christian maturity to be defined spiritually or culturally?

How Much of Worship is Cultural?

Music is inherently an expression of cultural preferences. Few liturgical partisans would deny this. But classic liturgy is different, many would say. It is timeless and rises above cultural differences.

Thus, the belief that historical liturgy is culturally neutral leads to the conviction that everyone should benefit from learning to appreciate it.

But isn't the basic nature of classic liturgical expression already a culture preference? A liturgy is a pre-determined plan for worship, and classic liturgies consist of pre-written words (rites, litanies, collects, etc.) to be read or recited, and pre-determined actions (rubrics) the participants agree to follow. Such reliance on pre-written words and actions emphasizes formality. Clearly, insistence on written liturgies is a rejection of informal plans that leave many details of words and actions undefined ahead of time.

Preference for formal (pre-determined) or informal (allowing for spontaneity and diversity) is a matter of taste as much as music or literary expression are. Some Christians are more comfortable with formality; others appreciate the flexibility of informality that allows for spontaneity. Lutherans, coming from Northern European cultures, have tended toward formality. But is having everything for worship written out ahead of time inherent in Lutheranism? Are spontaneous, from-the-heart prayers and comments of transition in the worship service inherently unLutheran?

What matters most are the words of Scripture. They need to be read or recited. But can the choice of those readings at times be left to the worship leader? Do they all need to be worked out ahead of time in elaborate pericopies, or assigned selections of reading. The preference to use selections determined and arranged by a distant committee certainly has its value. But it is a matter of taste as well. Using the same Scriptural words of praise sung to the same tune every Sunday, rather than changing words and music from week to week, is a cultural preference. There is certainly no theological mandate for relying on only a small fraction of the ways to praise God on Sunday.

The drive for having everything arranged and written out ahead of time is to assure "the best" in worship. Written prayers, preferably composed by someone with literary talent, will likely be more eloquent than prayers improvised at the moment by an ordinary minister, and most certainly than prayers by ordinary church members. Time-tested tradition refines and presents the best, and tradition should be written to be protected, according to this reasoning.

The supporting rationale for this version of "the best," applied also to music is that true worship should be something thoughtful, costly, and appropriate to the occasion. The seriousness of worship should lead to the insistence on avoiding the slipshod, the flippant, or certainly the frivolous in our approach to God.[12] So, to avoid less than "the best," it makes sense to turn to the experts, who presumably know how to sort out slipshod, glib expressions and to avoid practices that are lacking in due respect. They can be relied upon to commend the most elevated forms of worship, with literary eloquence and excellent music, that can be offered.

But aren't critically correct literary and musical expressions of "the best" in worship inherently culturally conditioned? Can one set of cultural preferences really support the best worship of people from a broad variety of cultural experiences who would gather before God? Is cultural excellence the way God judges quality of worship?

Should Worship Planning Be Left to the Experts?

Experts in liturgy and church music certainly have much to offer in presenting options for a congregation's worship. Specialists can serve a valuable purpose. But as war is said to be too important to a nation to be left to the generals, so one can claim that worship is too important to the life of a church to be left to specialists in the field. Can one trust that their priorities and preferences will be in the best interests of the variety of worshipers, or even the average worshiper, to whom a congregation wishes to minister?

There are reasons for caution.

While liturgical specialists would resist the comparison, they serve in effect as consultants to the leaders of worship in a congregation. Congregational leaders, especially the pastor, should carefully assess what they propose. As business and institutional leaders learn quickly, consultants have inherent limitations.

1) Experts can lose touch.

Gracia Grindal is one of those experts. An ELCA seminary professor, she had first-hand involvement in the revisions that went into *LBW*. In retrospect she saw many flaws in this specialist-led effort of the 1970's, and she was led to express them in an article.

Grindal observes that while the revisions went in one general direction, the culture was moving the opposite way. Thus, while "the makers of hymnals and liturgical services" were attempting to become more formal and less personal, the younger generation was demanding informality and personal experience in worship. Sunday morning thus "became more and more monochromatic in style even as the culture demanded more, and more colorful and varied styles."[13]

Losing touch happened not only with the younger generation, but, oddly, with the older, too. In pursuit of planned "coherence" around theological themes, the planners too often failed to provide coherence, or keep touch with icons of faith (such as "The Old Rugged Cross"). "The prejudices against 'pandering' to the consumer culture, and fears of entertainment evangelism or of having bad taste, too often prevent us from making 'coherent' connections which move people."

2) Experts often have a different agenda.

Prof. Grindal endorses the observation of Lutheran-rooted sociologist Peter Berger that in recent decades music and worship in churches have been the scene of *Kulturkamph*, or cultural war: "Protestant liturgocrats...rejected the received tradition and returned their communities back to the edenic idea of the unified church of the fourth century."

The cultural war of recent decades leading up to current worship tensions is basically one battle in the long struggle between high culture and popular culture in Lutheran history. As someone who knows from the inside, Grindal describes the agenda of the recent high-culture protagonists: "They want to change what the people like and have a prophet's air about them as they work to discredit the memory and faith of the people, regardless of results in outreach and mission."

Like many aspects of cultural tastes around us, church culture tends to go in cycles. When a whole movement proceeds "regardless of results in outreach and mission," it leaves a flank dangerously exposed. How exposed became apparent when decades of declining membership and attendance offered the setting for the popular-culture offensive of the Church Growth movement. A new group of specialists and experts emerged to set direction for church leaders, and the logic of their mission to "outsiders" inevitably put worship practices up for examination. The contemporary worship movement among Lutherans is a result. Will the popular culture of contemporary worship go too far? Possibly. Cultural tastes, after all, do go in cycles. But perhaps out of the discussions can come healthy agreement on what "too far" is and how a church will know it has not gone "far enough" in its ministry.

3) Worship specialists tend to prefer their own specialized culture.

In general, consultants have a way of recommending what they know best and what will advance their own interests. That's a fact of life. You can usually predict a consultant's advice based on his or her source of expertise. That's why it is good to seek advice from several different sources and then evaluate them.

The liturgical renewal movement that took hold in Lutheran churches in the 1950's-70's was primarily university and seminary led, relying especially on library research into worship practices from many centuries ago. The late-19th-century Oxford movement in England that was so influential on the early English language Lutheran orders of service was university-led, as indicated by its name. Inevitably, the orientation in such centers of advanced education is elitist, emphasizing the high culture in which their professors and leaders specialize.

The current contemporary worship movement has its base in congregations pursuing mission outreach to people not yet in the church. The source of expertise is not in past cultures but in observing effectiveness in current cultures. In the introductory chapter of this book, the story of development of contemporary worship at St. John Lutheran Church in Orange, California, was one of growing interest based on observations that "it works." Changes in worship practices increased the effectiveness of outreach to new people.

Such a source of expertise based on practice in ordinary culture is very different from expertise based on what appeals to high-culture specialists. That few Lutheran seminaries or colleges provide any

We at CSP need to address this?

kind of leadership for developing contemporary worship practices is not hard to understand. The cultural reference points are different and thus the expertise differs.

Such tension can be difficult to handle for people who want unambiguous answers. They usually prefer only one source. But tension can be healthy when it helps get the best fit of practices appropriate for specific people, places, and purposes. Whatever emerges in Lutheran churches in the decades ahead, worship is likely to improve because of contemporary challenges to classic practices and musical expressions. And the contemporary expressions will be richer because of the high standards set by classic worship resources.

4) Cross-cultural ministries call for different worship expertise.

The high culture and popular culture discussed so far have at least shared the English language—although they may use different dialects. The issue of expertise gets much more complicated when considering effective worship leadership for people most comfortable with other languages, which in effect represent other cultures. "Indigenization" is a term used to describe the process of encouraging Christians of other cultures to develop Gospel-based understandings, worship and church life in linguistic and musical expressions that best communicate and fit in their own particular culture. There is increasing awareness among Lutherans that this is a good thing to do, and in fact it is something that has historically happened whenever the cutting edge of Christianity pervaded new cultures.

A huge topic, indigenization of Christianity is something I refer to only to make a specific worship-related point. Commitment to spreading the Gospel to new people in different cultures means openness to the expertise of Christians who know those cultures and their special literary and musical expressions. This mission challenge necessitates broadening the base of worship expertise. Once this step is understood and taken for cultures with separate languages, why not follow the logic to indigenization within sub-cultures of English-language America? This is the direction in which the contemporary worship movement is headed.

The Restoration Story focused on the relatively easy task of reducing diversity by eliminating the separate ethnic heritages brought by Lutheran immigrants. This happened among Christians who implicitly gave assent to accepting English high church culture as their own.

The Other Story focuses on mission to people who are not ready to give such assent, usually because they have not yet developed the loyalty necessary to adapt themselves to this specialized church culture. Be they people who are most at home in a popular American sub-culture or people whose primary language means they know best a different culture, they are people to be reached with the Gospel. Advocates of the Other Story are inclined to see such outreach as a challenge Lutherans should accept as willingly as do other evangelistic Christian church bodies.

Lutheran church leaders in America have proven themselves effective at eliminating cultural diversity. Will some be allowed and even encouraged now to build on the older heritage of diversity in order to act on the challenge of reaching out to the diverse cultures of today?

---

[1] Eric Routley, *Music, Sacred and Profane*, London: Independent Press, 1960, p. 138.

[2] Richard John Neuhaus, "The Lutheran Difference: What's Really Wrong with the Church Growth Movement," *Lutheran Forum*, Reformation, 1990, p. 22.

[3] Ibid., p. 22.

[4] Calvin M. Johansson. *Discipling Music Ministry*, Hendrickson Publishers, 1992, p. 75.

[5] Ibid., p. 81.

[6] Ibid., p. 108.

[7] Ibid., p. 47.

[8] Ibid., p. 50.

[9] Ibid., p. 81.

[10] Ibid., p. 4

[11] Ibid., p. 113.

[12] Ralph P. Martin, *The Worship of God: Some Theological Pastor, and Practical Reflections*, Eerdmans, 1982, p. 19.

[13] Gracia Grindal, "Faithful in the Face of Change," *Word and World*, Vol XII, No 3, (Summer 1992), p. 223.

Chapter 8

Reference Points for Wisdom in Choosing Worship Practices

The Restoration Story that today dominates Lutheran understandings of worship traces its vision back to Henry Melchior Muhlenberg. This forceful 18th-century Lutheran leader dreamed of the day when all Lutheran congregations in North America would be united and would all use the same order of service.[1] How better to legitimize a movement than to trace its rationale back to the earliest prominent Lutheran in this country.

But even with such a seemingly simple beginning, that part, too, of the full story of Lutherans at worship has another side. The Other Story can trace roots to Muhlenberg, too. In addition to being a trained organist, he was foremost a missionary who understood the need to use the music and language of the people he was evangelizing. Wanting to reach out to Native Americans, he agreed with his Indian agent father-in-law that in order to convert them one would have "to learn the Indian melodies and tones and propagate the Law and Gospel with these tones so it would make an impression and then with God's blessing and help await the fruitage."[2]

Lutheran churches today face the same issue and tensions Muhlenberg recognized. It's good to have common identity and to do as much alike as possible. But the world we want to serve is big and full of diversity. Grass roots ministry opportunities and pressures keep raising exceptions that don't fit the mold fashioned for the time. The accommodation of diversity keeps tension on the vision for unity.

What would Muhlenberg make out of the contemporary worship movement today? Would he hold up *LBW* or *LW* and insist, This only and nothing else? Or would he be tuned into today's equivalent of Indian drums looking for ways to make an impression with the Gospel on new people?

We'll never know, of course. Nor can anyone claim with certainty what Martin Luther himself would do today. It's stimulating to speculate, though, especially in church bodies that carry the name of a 16th-century reformer as their identity. Is reformation a one-time event that provides a fixed heritage for a church body, or does the reforming repeat itself as churches age and experience changing circumstances?

How church leaders like Martin Luther and Henry Muhlenberg can serve especially well today is in modeling commitment to exercising wisdom in the complications of putting theology into practice. As outstanding leaders of their eras, they could respect and keep in tension competing pressures that came from diversity. They could emphasize the common ground and fashion unifying agreements that brought out the best in what fellow leaders had to offer in the different circumstances they faced. Regarding the worship tensions in Livonia, Luther's plea was for "good spiritual leaders who will know how to lead the people with wisdom and discretion."

So a Muhlenberg could strive for a common approach to worship but leave room for what works in a different culture, like that of Native Americans. Martin Luther could strive for order and structure in his city without insisting that all others in the Reformation do it the same way. And C. F. W. Walther in the 19th-century could probe with exquisite subtlety the implications for pastoral work of the proper distinction between Law and Gospel. This is, by the way, the same issue that is fundamental to the worship controversies of this day. These were outstanding leaders because they were wise.

What is the course of wisdom in choosing worship practices today? Right now leaders in hundreds of congregations across the land are probing for that wisdom. Pastors are in continuing discussions with young adults and mission-minded leaders about trying some contemporary practices. Pastors are also carrying on talks with elders who worry about offending long-time members if any changes are made. "We won't be Lutheran anymore," is a phrase heard now and then.

Hundreds, perhaps thousands of Lutheran pastors are seeking their own path of wisdom as they carry on conversation and prayer in their heads: "Should I explore going contemporary? (Or, now that we've started, how far should I go?) I hear most of the growing churches have broadened their approach to worship. But that's bound to make some of our strongest members unhappy. I'm not sure I have the skills. I can see my pastor-colleagues shaking their heads; they'll say I sold out. I ought to be defending our liturgy, like they do at seminary. Whatever we do, I want to be a faithful Lutheran. Lord what should we do?"

The chapters in this book are meant as a contribution to the ongoing search for wisdom in the many different situations Lutheran leaders face. There is no easy formula for following the logic of change and diversity while hanging on to a basic unity. One assumption, however, is uncomplicated and appropriate. Wisdom for worship planning will best emerge when leaders face the whole story of what is involved, when they broaden their understanding of the options from their heritage and for their mission possibilities.

Classic liturgical worship practices have many strengths. Otherwise how would they have become so dominant in Lutheran churches of our time? But, like any specific set of practices, they have weaknesses, too. For some purposes, other practices can be better suited. That's why there is and should be tension over worship planning and leadership. That's why there are few shortcuts on the difficult path of identifying worship wisdom for specific congregations.

Perspectives on Wisdom for Worship Leadership

Here are some perspectives on wisdom for leadership through the options and tensions of worship planning in Lutheran churches today.

1) **At present, wisdom for congregations and church bodies lies in the direction of accommodating diversity in worship practices.**

Expectations change from generation to generation. Limiting or eliminating diversity seemed wise and acceptable for several decades after the successes of the large-scale unified efforts of World War II. Budgets, charitable solicitations, and school districts were unified. And mergers in Lutheranism accelerated.

But few today would easily accept the notion that uniformly bigger and broader is necessarily better. In recent decades institutions from corporate businesses to schools to hospitals and some churches have been learning to offer those they serve more options to better accommodate individual preferences. An attitude of "take it or leave it" does not work well in most organized endeavors any more. From the perspective of religion, there are lots of things wrong with a consumer society. But that's what we are in. Common sense as well as wisdom point toward accommodating varied expectations as much as can be done within theological integrity.

Lutherans used to be very good at accommodating diversity in worship and church practices. Church life varied from region to region and language to language in Europe. Accommodation to various languages and customs seemed an obvious necessity in establishing Lutheranism in America. For many generations, adjusting to "primitivism" and "ethnicism," to use Luther Reed's pejorative labels, was a strength which could model how to recover new strength today. In the long run, the accelerated unification of Lutheran organizations and worship nationwide in the mid and late 20th-century may turn out to be an exception rather than the norm in Lutheran history.

To some leaders, "accommodation" may seem an undesirable concept, akin to selling out. The Apostle Paul did not think so. To the Corinthians he formulated the wisdom that guided his leadership in founding and overseeing churches.

> Though I am free and belong to no man, I make myself a slave to everyone, to win as many as possible. To the Jews I became like a Jew, to win the Jews. To those under the law I became like one under the law (though I myself am not under the law), so as to win those under the law. To those not having the law I became like one not having the law (though I am not free from God's law but am under Christ's law), so as to win those having the law. To the weak I became weak, to win the weak. I have become all things to all men so that by all possible means I might save some. I do all this for the sake of the gospel, that I may share in its blessings. (1 Cor 9:19-23)

Keep in mind Paul's commitment to become weak for the weak in finding wisdom for the worship controversies of today.

2) Wisdom lies in the direction of improving communication in church services.

The characteristics of contemporary worship discussed in the first chapter are all related to attempts to improve communication to people whose participation is not carried by habit or traditional loyalties. Communication describes the whole process of putting a message into sounds or writing, conveying those symbols and then having the recipients successfully receive and interpret what was intended.

At the simplest level, high-quality sound amplification of everything said or sung is an obvious improvement. Getting and holding the interest of the listeners is a prerequisite to delivering a message that lands and has impact. So is using words they understand without specialized training. The images of fast-paced television and the constant barrage of oral and print messages increasingly train people in our society to shorten their attention span and to turn off all but the most interesting communication attempts. The hurdle for communication in churches to be good keeps getting higher.

Wistful discussion can be heard among some pastors that the church goal is proclamation, not communication. But that's like trying to repeal the laws of gravity. Proclamation that does not get heard and applied is like preaching in German to people who only know English. Perhaps the Holy Spirit can do something, but he can work more effectively when at the human level proclamation first turns into communication.

We know the Holy Spirit wants to work through communication that is compelling and easily understood. That's why at Pentecost he gave the apostles the gift of all those different languages they found themselves speaking to people from those many different cultures. Most of those hearers could have gotten by with Greek or Hebrew. But the Holy Spirit obviously wanted to accommodate their needs and get on their wavelength as much as possible. He also led those apostles to make attention-getting spectacles of themselves in order to get and hold the attention of those to whom proclamation was to be made.

The Apostle Paul excelled at proclamation of the Gospel. But he also understood the importance of communication. When he addressed the Jews in the synagogues, he spoke from the Hebrew scripture. To increase his chances of communicating to the Greek philosophers in Athens, he spoke cultured Greek and cited their literature. To the common people in Jerusalem, he used the Aramaic dialect of Hebrew.

The English language today, has, in effect, many dialects of specialized vocabulary and connotations. The mission challenge in communicating the Gospel is to adapt the message to dialects and patterns of speech and music that present the fewest barriers to understanding by those to be reached and thereby the fewest human barriers to the Holy Spirit's work.

3. **Wisdom lies in the direction of purposefully assessing effectiveness of worship practices.**

While "effectiveness" is not a term commonly used in Lutheran discussion of worship, the concept becomes important when distinguishing between plans for worship and the actual worship event. Worship leaders committed to classic liturgy are ready to assess their plans by historical and literary standards. Worship participants can reasonably expect any worship plan, including the classic ones, to be assessed also for their effectiveness in bringing about desired outcomes in the actual event. This amounts to broadening the standard for evaluation.

Chapter 4 presented a number of Biblical references that can be used for assessing what happens in worship events. Some, like presenting the Word of God richly, can be adequately provided for by careful use of scripts. But other outcomes have to be assessed based on experiences of the actual event. Wise worship leaders would want to incorporate feedback from participants into exploration of options for improvement.

4) **Wisdom lies in the direction of readiness to adjust to cultural changes.**

The change of primary concern is not in the worship service but in the culture that is shaping those who would worship. The driving force of rapid technological development is having strong ripple effects on the everyday ways people experience life.

The distinction between the cultural environment of a camp in contrast to a village has proven helpful.[3] Traditional Lutheran worship developed in a village setting characterized by permanence in relationships. Membership in the parish overlapped with residence in the village, and widespread familiarity with church routines could be assumed. Now most people in our current culture, especially in urban areas, live within temporary relationships like that of a camp where people come and go, and church culture is not a primary part of life for most.

One response to cultural change is to concentrate on preserving islands of constancy. Traditional Lutheran worship can do this for those who know its ways and appreciate the village sense of permanence. But outreach to those in the predominately unchurched culture calls for adapting to expectations of people who approach life like a camp of temporary relationships and who do not have the patience to slowly absorb village strengths. Contemporary worship usually incorporates attempts to adjust to camp-like culture.

Most Lutheran congregations do not have to choose one approach at the expense of the others. They can pursue the best of both worlds by following traditional, classic worship practices in one service and by pursuing contemporary music and practices in another.

5) Wisdom lies in the direction of separating issues of style from matters of substance.

Whether to use music with four-part harmony or to have a freer-flowing left hand accompaniment is a question of style. Insisting on presenting God's initiatives that bring the response of worship is a matter of substance. The importance of distinguishing between substance and style was elevated in my book *Evangelical Style and Lutheran Substance* (1988). Its focus was on styles of speaking and organizing, and the chapters about talking had implications for worship.

In the years since that publication I have engaged in many pastoral-conference dialogues with various defenders of traditional Lutheran style who insist that Lutheran substance necessitates this style. I have a hard time replicating their arguments, which seem to be variations on the theme, It just has to be this way.

My main point is that every church draws a line between what cannot change within faithfulness to their identity, and what can change and take various forms. The first is the church's substance, and the changeable amounts to style. Some church leaders want to draw a very big circle around what they do and call it substance. But we can learn from the very first leaders of the Christian church, like James, Peter, and Paul, that wisdom lies with keeping the circle around substance as small as possible, to allow for variations in style. Their council that established this principle is recorded in Acts 15. Their guiding concern was, "We should not make it difficult for the Gentiles who are turning to God" (Acts 15:19).

In the current discussions the equivalent of non-Jewish Gentiles are people who did not grow up with Lutheran traditions. How much of the traditions do they have to learn to appreciate in order to be served by churches with doctrinal convictions emphasized by Lutherans? One would hope no more than necessary to get to the Gospel substance.

6: Wisdom lies in the direction of testing new styles to see what happens.

Especially in worship, the fundamental leadership question is how well the Holy Spirit can work through the various ways Word and sacraments can be presented. Will God's blessings be on a new style that is tried out as well as or better than on the old? How people respond and who they are has to be part of that assessment. So long as the substance of God's initiatives conveyed by his Word are presented, can the risk be too great to run for the sake of mission outreach?

This kind of decision is like the one faced by the keepers of Jewish tradition when faced by the activity of the followers of Jesus Christ. Gamaliel expressed wisdom worth hearing today: "Therefore, in the present case I advise you: Leave these men alone! Let them go! For if their purpose or activity is of human origin, it will fail. But if it is from God, you will not be able to stop these men" (Acts 5:38,39). Should advocates of contemporary worship emerge in a congregation, leaders would be wise to find opportunity to let them try. If God blesses this effort, rejoice. Your church may be on the way to offering the advantages of both old and new styles.

Some Theological Parameters To Guide the Selection of Worship Practices

Previous chapters have highlighted various principles and parameters of theological signficiance that can productively guide discussion of worship practices at local and synodical levels of Lutheran churches. In summary:

A. Lutherans confess that worship practices can be different between and within congregations. These are external matters of indifference (adiaphora). Done in an orderly way, each congregation can change, reduce, or increase ceremonies as it see fit, to achieve its mission. Unity in doctrine is not disrupted by diversity in worship practices. Thus worship practices and styles are the wrong part of church life on which to try to force church unity. (See pages 61-64 and 68 in this book.)

B. The "soul" of Lutheranism is centrality of the doctrine of justification by grace through faith. This standard prohibits legalistic approaches to establishing worship practices. Only when resistance to change turns into liturgical legalism can the current discussions be considered a struggle for the basic identity of Lutheranism. Lutherans faithful to the confessions must recognize Christian liberty in matters of worship. (See pages 67-68).

C. Confidence in justification by grace through faith rests on the objective certainty of God's promises conveyed in Word and sacraments. Thus Lutheran worship needs to feature these means of grace. Preaching and teaching God's Word is of necessity the main part of all divine service. The sacrament of the Lord's Supper is a precious means of grace to be highly appreciated, but a rationale for featuring it in every Lutheran divine service is neither theologically nor historically compelling. (See pages 49-50 and 93-95).

D. Lutheran worship should include subjective response to God's initiatives conveyed in his Word. As the Large Catechism says, "They assemble to hear and discuss God's word and to praise God with song and prayer." Worshipers come both to be strengthened in faith and to express their faith. This dual purpose brings a tension into worship planning that needs to be maintained.

Confusion about the importance of response arises because the English word "worship" is now used in a broad sense that covers everything happening during public assembly in a divine service. The narrow sense of response to God's initiatives is consistent with Scriptural words translated as worship. Contemporary "praise and worship" music approaches worship in the narrow sense. Concern for the subjective response of heartfelt worship should lead to assessing effectiveness of worship practices. (See pages 56-58)

E) A basic concern in selection of specific worship practices should be providing for the weak. Luther was clear that the choice of worship forms is not a matter of personal preference, but should depend on the needs of others. In relation to ceremonies, the Formula of Concord instructs that we can in good conscience yield to the weak. (See pages 69-71)

Proponents of highly formal, classic worship plans often present them as for mature Christians, as if the appeal to maturity should be the major concern. But this rationale is not the most appropriate. As the Apostle Paul teachs, "we who are strong ought to bear with the failings of the weak and not to please ourselves" (Romans 15:1). More appropriate for worship leaders is to make special provision for the weak. These include those who are coming to faith and entering the fellowship as well as those whose weakness is dependence on traditional forms. Most congregations can accommodate both sets of weaknesses through provision of different worship services.

Keep the Discussion Spiritual

The public assembly of Christians for divine service is a special workplace for the Holy Spirit. The Word and sacraments are the means by which he comes to participants to convey the Gospel of Christ to each. When he connects, he works responses of faith that lead to heartfelt thankfulness, praise, and (used in the narrow sense) worship.

Without denying the Spirit's power to work his way, we can observe that he connects better with certain people in some settings and practices than he does in others. People differ in the needs, experiences, expectations, and weaknesses they bring to a Sunday service. Thus it seems prudent to use several different plans for offering the means of grace and opportunities for participants to respond. As we have seen, Lutheran worship leaders have such freedom and even a mandate to address various weaknesses.

Still, despite our best human planning, we are dependent on the Holy Spirit for the spiritual impact of that hour or so together. This is the same Spirit of wisdom that guides followers of Christ in their decision making within and for the body of Christ. Whatever happens in debate and in formulation of worship policy, there should be repeated and fervent prayer to God the Father to send his Spirit richly upon those who look for his will in the options they face. It is hard to imagine how congregation members and especially worship leaders could go very far in addressing differing perspectives on worship without frequent pauses to pray for the Spirit's guiding presence.

Worship should be in spirit and in truth. So should the discussion about practices for doing it. The truth for a specific congregation emerges best from considering all the relevant perspectives. The Spirit comes from keeping the discussion grounded in the Word of God and by staying open to his movement. Whatever else, keep the worship debates spiritual.

---

[1] Luther Reed, *The Lutheran Liturgy*, Muhlenberg, 1959, p. 182.

[2] Gracia Grindel, "Faithful in the Face of Change," *Word and World,* Vol XII, No. 3, (Summer 1992), p. 225.

[3] David S. Luecke, *Evangelical Style and Lutheran Substance*, Concordia, 1988, pp 51-62.